MAKING IT HAPPEN

MAKING IT HAPPEN

The Unit President Concept

J. Keith Louden

American Management Association, Inc.

International standard book number: 0-8144-5260-4
Library of Congress catalog card number: 73-152879

Fourth Printing

To
Genevieve S. Louden
and my many colleagues
who made it all possible

Foreword

WHEN we discuss management we often say that the unique asset of a company is its people.

Yet the problem of involving them in the operation and planning of a company so that they are motivated to give of their best and are committed to its objectives is one that has long concerned most students and practitioners of management. J. Keith Louden has been keenly aware of the importance of the individual employee and his participation in group effort. He records in this book his experiences and philosophy concerning this vital aspect of successful management practice.

He believes completely that it is both possible and essential that the individual employee not lose his identity in the organization. By participation in this management effort of the company, he can enhance his personal development and realize a high degree of satisfaction from his own contribution.

It is through participation that an employee's job is put in a new light. He sees things differently vis-à-vis management. A competitive relationship tends to shift to a cooperative one. If he is consulted he becomes aware of a mutual interdependence.

If the employees have nothing to say about the way things are done, they are likely to show little interest or concern. They drift along on the job, content to "get by" while doing as little as they can. But when they are involved in solving problems connected with their jobs they join wholeheartedly in finding the solutions.

The author believes that the manager who encourages participative methods will succeed best in the face of changes that surround American organizations.

This is an interesting and thoughtful book. As a behavioral scientist and professional manager, I commend it to you for reading and study.

Alfred J. Marrow

Preface

IN professional management, individual ability and effectiveness play a very important part. Yet the vital element in the success of any organization is the manager's skill in developing a team which blends individual abilities and know-how to bring about a result that could not be achieved in any other way. The professional manager does not simply hope this will happen; he makes it happen.

Although the ability to involve the total group in the managerial effort is paramount to its success, concern is expressed on every side that members of management, particularly those in the lower echelon, do not seem to feel committed to the company effort. It is my judgment that this is not an innate lack of interest on their part, but results from upper management's lack of ability to involve them in the processes and practices of management to the point where they feel as concerned with the end results as, say, the chief executive.

The purpose of this book is to describe a way of accomplishing the total involvement which results in total commitment. It will concentrate on two premises: first, the importance to the individual of developing to his greatest potential, and second, the involvement of the total team in the management processes of the company so that there is a unified commitment to the agreed-upon objectives. The book's approach represents a combination of philosophy and practices as well as a case history. It develops the concept of total involvement in depth in the organization and supports it by detailing the practices which will help to bring it about.

As I began writing, my mind was crowded with experiences and with the images of the people I have worked with over the years. Many of these men and women had a profound impact upon my thinking and understanding and my dedication to professional management. To give all their names would be an impossible task; nevertheless, I do want to mention two. Ralph C. Davis, now professor emeritus at Ohio State University, first brought home to me while I was a student there the importance of management as a profession and the role it must play in the future. To say it another way, he opened my eyes to what management is and set my feet on the path which was to result in a most rewarding career. I am also profoundly indebted to the late Arthur E. Rauch, my superior when I joined the Owens Illinois Glass Company in Toledo, Ohio. It was Art Rauch who first demonstrated to me the effectiveness of the systematic, analytical approach to the solution of management problems and drilled into me permanently the importance of searching out and dealing with facts rather than prejudices and opinions in the solution of managerial problems.

So with these two specific references, I give a deep and affectionate bow to all those who made such a great contribution to my own personal development—even those whose chief contribution was to teach me how not to manage, which in itself is a form of learning. Naturally, I remember them with less affection.

J. Keith Louden

Contents

1

The Challenge

I know you mean it when you say that we are all members of the management team, but we just don't feel it. In our own areas of responsibility we know fairly well what to do, but we don't always understand why. It's not really a problem of communications; it's a feeling that we don't know the objectives of the company because we aren't in on the decisions. Programs are handed to us to carry out, and we don't know what the thinking is behind them, or how to go about developing programs ourselves. We want to belong to the kind of management team you have in mind, but how can we do it?

IN essence this foreman's question challenges top management to stop talking about modern management and start practicing it. It is a challenge that is rarely voiced;

1

more often, the principles of participative management are enthusiastically accepted by everyone and then, with everyone's tacit consent, left to fade away down the line.

The foreman in this case spoke up because he had become convinced that top management in our company, which I shall call the YAC Corporation, really intended to decentralize authority. But, as his comments indicate, turning the theory into reality requires much more than intellectual assent, and the real work was still ahead of us. This book is the story of that work, how hard it was, how exciting it was, and how it paid off.

Plateau in Growth

A medium-sized manufacturer of consumer durables and industrial mechanical equipment, the YAC Corporation had hit a growth plateau in the late 1940s and early 1950s, as a result had lost its place as No. 1 in the industry, and now in the mid-fifties was in danger of losing the No. 2 position. Product reputation was high, and the company was well accepted in the field. But YAC had failed to keep pace in a growing economy, primarily because it was not organized to take advantage of such growth. It was a tightly centralized operation which for 30 years had been controlled by one man.

That man, the president and chief executive officer, was unquestionably the best engineer, best salesman, and best financial officer the company had. He had brought YAC successfully through the Depression with only one loss quarter, and that a minor one. He had attracted good men, and they performed well under him. But he had never learned to delegate the authority that would have enabled them to make their greatest contribution.

The president reserved so many powers to himself that even his top executives were hardly a management team. He called them into meetings to arrive at decisions that they should have handled themselves, and he expected them to submit all projects for his approval. This was difficult to do because he was so often out of his office: he might be found in the engineering department tinkering with a product design, or out in the field helping to close a sale, or working at some other job around the plant. With these methods of operating, the growth of the company was geared to his ability to be nimbly on the spot everywhere that decisions had to be made.

With these methods too, the functions of the company had become compartmentalized structures that were uncoordinated except in the person of the president. As a consequence the functions often worked against each other, as when the engineering department designed products that did not really meet marketing needs or take full account of manufacturing costs.

The president did try to arbitrate between the functions, and he made attempts to delegate some of his powers. It was all a sometime effort, however, since his executives were not accustomed to thinking in terms of overall objectives. They were untrained in accepting authority and inexperienced in exercising it. They could never be sure how long it would last or even how sincerely it was offered, so that the safest course was to continue referring decisions up the line.

Eventually the president together with his board of directors realized that the company's lack of progress made a change essential, not only in the corporate idea of management but in its practice throughout the organization. And they decided that because of his inherent tendencies to run a one-man show, the president should not attempt to carry out such a change himself.

It was at this point that I was brought into YAC as an outsider who was incapable of being the best engineer, best salesman, and best everything else in the company. One of the few areas that I knew well was management, and I was given responsibility for leading the transition from a highly centralized organization to a decentralized, delegated-authority structure.

Two Pilot Projects

When I joined YAC, many members of its management knew me only by reputation. It seemed wise, therefore, not to assume full authority immediately but to give myself time to learn something about the business and demonstrate my ability for getting things done. As an initial step I decided to concentrate on two of the company's major problems. The first was inventory: It was too high, particularly in finished goods, and it was seriously out of balance in relation to actual sales needs. The second was the coordination of product design among the engineering, sales, and manufacturing departments. Owing to the isolation of each function that had developed, sales and manufacturing seldom saw the next season's product line until the designs were completed. At this point any suggestions for changes led to a battle and delayed the start of production.

Study of the inventory problem identified three contributing factors:

- Almost total lack of communication between sales and manufacturing.
- An annual sales forecast that was looked upon as unchangeable. (The vice-president of marketing's stock phrase was "You make them, we'll sell them.")
- Virtually no recognition of the impact of actual versus predicted sales.

The solution was simple enough, although it took time to implement. We formed a new group, the operations planning department, and gave it full authority over all manufacturing schedules and all elements of inventory related to products. The general company policy that the group was to carry out was stated concisely: "Inventory shall be controlled to the minimum investment required to meet actual sales and minimum costs." The new department then established an orderly procedure for inventory administration, with weekly meetings that coordinated sales forecasts compared with actual sales, and production plans compared with actual production needs.

When the procedure went into effect, the impact of changing production schedules was severe as actual sales results were fed into the process. The imbalance flowed back into work in process and into the raw materials

5

inventory. Since purchasing schedules were also affected, it flowed back to the company's suppliers as well. As we struggled to meet actual sales needs while sharply reducing the finished goods inventory, manufacturing costs were adversely affected by the changing production schedules and shorter runs.

It was a painful but necessary experience, and the departments faced up to it without hesitation. The results in inventory investment were soon large enough to be noted with approval by the board of directors and the banks. The price we paid in earnings was disagreeable but not disastrous. And, after the initial period of adjustment, the sensitive controls we had established kept inventory in a healthy condition both in the plant and on the books.

The second problem, that of coordinating product design, was resolved in a similar manner. We set up teams consisting of representatives from sales, manufacturing, engineering, and cost accounting to establish perimeters for all specifications and costs before the design cycle began. So that nothing would be left to chance, we developed what we called a laboratory-to-production schedule which specified by model numbers what steps were to be taken by what dates. The schedule insured that inputs from the various groups would be received while they could still be modified without creating problems of redesign.

As it turned out, the most important contributions made by this system were, first, that it got everyone into the act who belonged there and, second, that it set up a schedule for results which enforced the cutoff date: When a design was frozen, *it was frozen*. This fact alone materially reduced the number of nervous breakdowns suffered in each design season.

Although by working out these problems we freed the company of some major handicaps, the solutions were neither complex nor mysterious. All we did was to apply sound management principles and proven practices to bring order where it was needed. As for my own standing in the company, after the four months that I spent in developing the two programs I was well accepted by management and made a smooth transition into full operating responsibility.

Beginning the Change

As the new operating head and No. 2 man at YAC, for several months I led discussions of our alternatives, sometimes in sessions with top management, sometimes in general meetings of all management levels. The foreman's comment given earlier was typical in that the willingness to change was there, but the know-how and courage to do so were not. To develop a decentralized operation we had to arrive at a uniform concept of the best way our particular business could be managed. Then we had to work out a plan of implementation fitted to our circumstances. We decided early that we must do these things ourselves—that while we would use outside specialists in some areas, we were the ones who knew the total situation and should stay with it.

Since it was our objective to be a more profession- ally managed company, we examined what we believed management to be. We agreed that when we are managing, we are planning, organizing, controlling, or motivating. When we are not doing one of these, we are doing something ourselves; therefore, we are operating. We realized that all levels of management inevitably perform some functions themselves, the actual amount increasing inversely in relation to the management hierarchy. That is, the president may spend about 90 percent of his time in managing and 10 percent in operating, while a first-line supervisor may perform operating tasks 60 or 70 percent of the time (see Exhibit 1-1). We agreed that it is important to distinguish between the things we are getting done through other people—by managing—and the things we are doing ourselves—by operating.

We wanted to be certain that all work performed, of a direct or an indirect nature, made a recognizable contribution toward reaching our objectives. Nothing was to be done because someone thought it a good idea or because other companies did it. We all agreed that we had too much actual work to accomplish to engage

Exhibit 1-1. Managing versus operating.

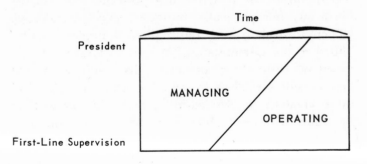

in window dressing or wheel spinning. We also wanted the work that we performed to be done in the simplest way we could devise and assigned to the lowest level at which a person could be fully accountable for it.

If we were to achieve company objectives, we knew that we would have to get our employees committed to them. And we decided that the best way to do this was by consultative or participative management—that is, by involving everyone in setting the objectives of his group. In the process, everyone would have to understand how his group's objectives were related to those of the group above him and to the corporate goals.

We wanted our people to be creative and imaginative in fulfilling their responsibilities—to exercise self-supervision, self-control, and self-appraisal. But before they could do so they would need to know exactly what their job was, what authority they had to carry it out, and what results were acceptable. Therefore, our definitions of job areas must be clear and complete from the beginning; no one should have to ask what was expected of him.

Carrying this thinking to its conclusion, we realized that if we were to achieve decentralization of responsibility, authority, and accountability, people at every level of the organization must "think like a president." They would have to accept the same kind of responsibility for results in their areas that a president does for the company as a whole. They must carry out their functions as if they held the ultimate authority at the point where the buck stops (see Exhibit 1-2).

This approach was accepted with enthusiasm by a

9

Exhibit 1-2. The unit president concept *(this chart illustrates the concept and is not intended to reflect the total organization of the company).*

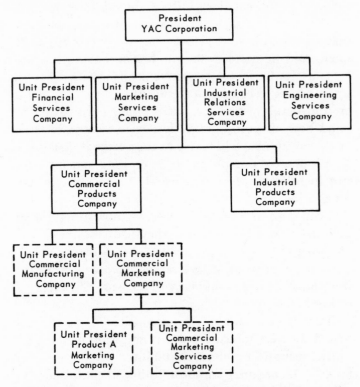

majority in the company, but so far it was still just talk. Before we could meet the challenge of introducing the techniques of professional management, we had to stop talking and start doing. At all levels policies, plans, and procedures had to be formulated, accepted by the people concerned, coordinated, and put into writing. The boundaries of each person's area of responsibility had to be defined, and within this area his authority and standards of performance specified. The following chapters spell out how we did it. After three years of hard work we had not moved YAC to the top of the industry, but we had consolidated the No. 2 position. Above all, in the process we had doubled sales and tripled profits.

2

The Unit President: Defining the Boundaries

IN order to provide our unit presidents with maximum freedom for decision making and innovation, we had to set specific limits to their operations. The combination of freedom and restraint may seem to be contradictory, but in practice a manager must know exactly what his area of responsibility is before he can work inside it with the creativity that stems from confidence. To decentralize authority in the YAC Corporation we undertook to build a fence around each job, making the area of activity as broad as possible to encourage maximum participation and creativity but specifying the boundaries unmistakably.

As shown in Exhibit 2-1, we decided that one side of the fence would be an outer limit relating primarily to the world at large—customers, vendors, the community, government, and other outside agencies—while the other three sides would be boundaries within the company. For side 1, the outer boundary, we wanted to define our attitudes and practices concerning matters of law, morals, and ethics. Side 2, the first of the three "inside" perimeters, would specify plans and the policies behind them. Side 3 would outline the unit president's responsibilities—not only his assigned duties, but also the authority he had to carry them out and the standards of performance that would be considered acceptable. Side 4, control, was to include budgets, standard procedures, and the information that he would need for control.

Obviously the construction of these fences is a major effort in any company. They cannot be decided on by an appointed group and then turned over to the people who occupy the jobs; everyone must help to develop his

Exhibit 2-1. The boundaries.

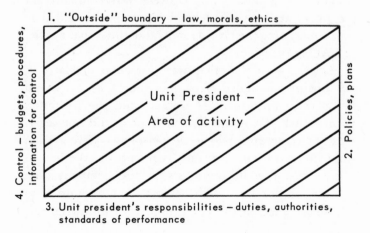

1. "Outside" boundary — law, morals, ethics

4. Control — budgets, procedures, information for control

Unit President — Area of activity

2. Policies, plans

3. Unit president's responsibilities — duties, authorities, standards of performance

13

own boundaries. The participation of the people concerned was the secret of the unit president concept's success at YAC: They were involved in setting up the concept, they came to understand it thoroughly, and they committed themselves to making it work.

In the process of building the fences, the entire business was open for study, and many new approaches emerged. We developed a different way of going to market, changed from a functional to a divisional type of organization, separated certain manufacturing functions for more efficient production, and eliminated some product lines and added others. Defining the four boundaries shown in Exhibit 2-1 was an effective way to put every practice and every segment of the company under the microscope.

Side 1. The Outside Boundary

For the boundary line between our company and the world at large, we defined our attitudes and practices concerning the laws, morals, and ethics that applied to YAC's operations.

Laws. Legislation that was particularly related to our business included wage and hour laws, laws regulating the employment of women, and the Robinson-Patman Act. We found that most of us did not regard these as something which we personally were responsible for understanding and living up to. We had assumed that certain specialists in the company were accountable for its legal behavior: the corporate counsel, for instance, or the vice-president of industrial relations. Yet, when we began to analyze our operations from the legal standpoint, we realized that the decisions our managers made on the spot sometimes came under the jurisdiction of the law without their knowledge. In giving a routine authorization for overtime work, for example, a foreman would break the law because he was unaware that there is a legal limit to the number of hours women may work in a day.

If our managers were truly to act as presidents of their units, they had to know the law in their areas of responsibility. Although learning it was hard work for everyone, for the first time we all began to consider legal requirements as a routine factor in line decisions.

Morals. We agreed that there must be a moral code or tone in the company which governs the actions and attitudes of its employees. We also recognized that if managers are to be leaders of men they must be respected as men, not just as managers. Since a manager lives in a goldfish bowl, and since people tend to imitate the leader, he must do his best to be the kind of leader that he himself would want to follow. When we analyzed what we considered our personal rights and liberties, we found that many of them must be subjected to the total requirements of serving as a professional manager.

Ethics. Although we began our discussion of this area by talking about business ethics, we came to the conclusion that there is no such thing; there are only ethics that apply to all activities in our social system. We knew that our customers, our employees, our vendors, our stockholders, and the community at large were continually forming opinions about YAC which to-

15

gether made up their image of the company. Before we could regulate our actions, we needed to decide what images we wanted to project.

For example, what image did we want our vendors to have of our purchasing policies and practices? Could they trust us to preserve the confidential nature of their quotations and bids? Did we protect them on their disclosure of proprietary information and practices? Could they depend on us to be fair in our presentations for claims and allowances? Did we ask for special favors that turned out to be expensive for them? Did we try to upgrade agreed-upon specifications without acknowledging that we were increasing their costs?

When we explored such questions, we uncovered practices that were not in keeping with the image we wanted people to have of YAC. We carried this type of analysis through all elements of the business, after which it was a simple matter to write down our intentions as brief codes of ethics. These were statements of intent that, when we lived up to them, would cause people to have the image of us we wanted them to have.

Side 2. Policies and Plans

Policies. We agreed that policies are the rules of the game—decisions made in anticipation of need. At YAC, top management established corporate policy and put it into simple written form as statements of intent. Managers at every level then worked out for their own functions brief policy guidelines that conformed to the corporate policy. I believe that, when people understand the intent of policy, they will govern themselves much more effectively within policy than they will if we try to cover all possibilities in detail.

In the area of marketing, for example, a possible guideline might read: "It is our policy to confine our marketing activities to the continental United States." This sets a limit on the marketing manager. He has the right to challenge the policy and to supply data showing why he thinks it should be changed; but, as long as the policy remains in effect, he must follow it.

In the area of personnel relations, one guideline adopted by YAC stated: "It is our policy that we will promote from within the organization." Any hirings from the outside to fill vacancies were therefore a violation of policy and had to be approved by the person with the power to do so.

Plans. To carry out the policies, managers at every level prepared detailed plans. For example, the policy of promoting from within was implemented by a manpower planning procedure that included position descriptions, standards of performance, progress reviews, and individual manager development programs. Formal procedures that were established for recording and evaluating a man's potential indicated the areas in which he might be promoted and gave a timetable showing when he would be ready for consideration (these are discussed in Chapter 8).

Like policy making, planning began at the top and moved downward. Each unit president participated in setting the objectives of the larger unit over him and worked with his people to establish his own objectives. In addition, the planning groups prepared detailed descriptions of the steps that would lead from where they were to where they wanted to be. Since people do govern themselves more effectively when they know the intent of a policy, every unit president took time to make sure that his subordinates understood the purpose underlying the plan as well as to involve them in developing the plan itself.

Side 3. Unit President's Responsibilities—Definition

Position descriptions. To successfully practice the philosophy of decentralization, every member of the management team must know exactly what he is responsible for and what authority he has to carry out that responsibility. Accordingly, position descriptions were written to cover the following questions: What is the purpose of the job? What is its scope? What duties and responsibilities have been delegated to it? What powers have been granted? To whom does the employee report? Who reports to him? With whom does he work closely? The answers were carefully drawn up to prevent gaps or overlaps, either between superior and subordinate or between people who worked together.

Standards of performance. We defined standards as the results which the superior and subordinate agree beforehand will be considered acceptable. Once they are established, the unit president can work with confidence in the knowledge of his goals. The standards that we set at YAC covered each assigned responsibility and were put in quantitative form wherever possible. Thus the unit president was in a position to practice self-appraisal and self-control. Every employee's performance was reviewed regularly with him to measure it against the standards.

Side 4. Control

Budgets. Since a unit president's budget specifies the fiscal standards and results expected of him, it was worked out with him so that he understood it and felt it belonged to him. He was particularly involved in the elements of cost that he directly influenced—labor, materials, supplies, production quotas, overtime, waste, and the like. The standards we helped him establish in these areas were variable not only as to rate of activity but as to product mix. We wanted him to have budget standards and supporting data that were truly valuable in planning his daily operation. This meant that they had to reflect actual conditions and enable him to adjust quickly and effectively to a changing situation. Thus operations were preplanned to the maximum degree.

Procedures. We prepared standard procedures, or standard practice instructions, describing the simplest way to carry out repetitive functions. These were developed mainly by the people performing the function, since they were the ones who had to believe in the practices outlined and make them work. Our descriptions of the procedures were bound looseleaf for convenience in improving them, simplifying them, or even eliminating them.

Information for control. We decided on the data that would be required for control by asking the following questions: What information do the unit president and his superior need so that they will know whether events are conforming to plan? When do they need it? And in what form will it be most helpful?

We reviewed carefully with each unit president the vital elements of work he was responsible for that required careful control if he was to meet his objectives. We decided exactly what information would be most helpful to him to tell him how he was doing—in time to take corrective action early if his results were falling behind plan. This information was to be prepared with little attention to neatness or format but with high regard for accuracy and fast feedback.

Building the Fence

These were the four sides of the fences that we built in order to introduce participative management at the YAC Corporation. Work on this huge project started at the top, where I directed a policy committee composed of the men reporting to me. The group included representatives of every element of the business. It met once a week to decide basic policy, review actions taken and recommendations made by the working groups under it, and make assignments for the next week. Differences of opinion were resolved in these meetings, and fundamental issues such as the degree of decentralization practical were talked out and put into writing.

For differences of opinion we found it valuable to have an outside management consultant attend the meetings and act as an arbitrator. Repeatedly, when our viewpoints seemed irreconcilable, he was able to point out the basic agreement between us and help us bring the issue to a close. This was the only management consultant we employed in the course of reorganization, but without him the entire project might have been deadlocked or unduly influenced by my opinions.

The day after a policy group session, each of its members met with his own subordinates to review policy decisions and answer questions. Leaders of these groups were careful to take time for full discussion, since points were sometimes raised that needed to be sent to the top group for review. Then they developed their work program for that week. At lower levels, as many other working groups were formed as was necessary in order to involve every employee. The further down the line, of course, the narrower the scope of the studies. For example, a schedule clerk in the production control department served as a member of a team analyzing scheduling and production control procedures. It was through this companywide structure that we were able to examine everything in the business to determine, first, whether it was important; second, what contribution it made toward reaching our objectives; and, third, whether it could be done in a simpler way, assigned to a lower level of the organization, or eliminated completely. Equally important, everyone became involved.

Introducing Changes

As we began to decide on the changes we would make in the company, we set up a transition procedure

21

designed to minimize disruption. We did not save all changes for a certain date; they were introduced individually where possible. Implementation took the following form:

1. A large-scale comparative process flow chart of the new and old procedures was drawn and hung on the wall for discussion.
2. Employees who were directly involved analyzed the new procedure from the standpoints of need, effectiveness, flexibility, simplicity, and clarity.
3. The changes were then explained to employees who were indirectly involved. Their questions and objections were invited, and their acceptance was gained.
4. A step-by-step plan for introducing the new procedure was developed. It showed what action was to be taken, who was to take it, when it was to be taken, and what checks would be made to insure satisfactory performance.
5. If the change was a large one, frequently the old and the new procedures were run parallel until everyone was satisfied that the new method fulfilled all needs.

In this top-to-bottom reorganization of the firm it took us over a year to develop our first total structure. We worked nights, Saturdays, and Sundays and still carried on business as usual. We regarded it not as a sacrifice but as an opportunity to make YAC the company we thought it should be. We were totally absorbed in the effort, and this is one reason why it succeeded.

3

The Professional Manager

WHILE decentralization of the YAC Corporation was still in the discussion stage, we clarified our ideas about the management approach that we expected from ourselves and our unit presidents. We agreed that management is a profession, a discipline encompassing a specialized body of knowledge and techniques. The most important fact in the use of a management technique, however, is its impact on human performance. The job of the professional manager is to get things done through other people; therefore, his function is not the direction of things but the development of people. The greatest contribution he can make is to help his subordinates reach their highest potential, thus reducing the difference between actual and planned performance.

We agreed that the professional manager differs from most other professionals in that he can be an expert in the techniques of his field—for example, in production control or accounting—yet fail in his job because he cannot work with people or motivate them. The testing ground of his ability is the workplace: He must be able to act as a leader, to motivate, to make his people work hard and well because they want to, not because they have to. If he also has a profound understanding of the techniques and elements of management, he is a professional manager in the total sense.

We accepted this definition: "Management is taking things and people and molding them into dynamic organization units which achieve their objectives to the satisfaction of those served and with a high degree of morale and sense of attainment on the part of those rendering the service."

To paraphrase that definition, you could say that management is taking people and physical things and resources—molding and forming them into dynamic, live, vital organization units or teams which attain their objectives (with the emphasis on the word "their," since they were involved in the determination of what the objectives should be) to the satisfaction of those served, thus gaining their goodwill, and with a high degree of morale and sense of attainment on the part of those participating—which means they have the satisfaction of a job well done, a sense of belonging to a team, and a sense of purpose and of responsibility that they can gain in no other way.

Elements of Management

There is sometimes confusion between the elements and the functions of management. For the purposes of this book, the functions of management are marketing, manufacturing, finance, industrial relations, and the like. The elements of management are the four already named in Chapter 1: planning, organizing, controlling, and motivating.

Planning

Planning, the primary element that precedes all others, calls for conscious choices between alternative courses of action—considered judgments based on purposes, facts, and estimates. It is the job of making things happen that would not happen otherwise. Planning offers a systematic means by which a company can become what it wants to become. It is preparatory to action by people. It calls for establishing objectives, policies, procedures, and action programs.

Objectives. These are the goals of the firm. There must be objectives for each element or segment of the business, and the total of these equals the corporate objectives. For example, a corporate objective might be "It is our objective to achieve a return on investment of 6 percent after taxes." A marketing objective might be "It is the objective of the marketing function to increase sales to $50 million next year." Moving down the line in marketing, a narrower objective might be "In the service department, return calls for imperfect repairs will not exceed one in twenty."

Policies. As discussed in Chapter 2, policies are simple statements of general intent that serve as guides for achieving the objectives. They map out the field of action and build the areas of action. They are written for all levels, beginning with major policies applicable to the firm as a whole and proceeding through departmental policies to minor policies for small units. They must be consistent at all levels of the organization. An example given in Chapter 2 was "It is our policy to confine our marketing activities to the continental United States." Others might be "It is our policy that any one customer must not account for more than 15 percent of our total sales volume." "We will provide companywide promotion opportunities for our people." "We want at least two vendors for all key materials and components."

Procedures. As shown back in Exhibit 2-1, procedures are essentially a form of control. They are discussed here under planning because they mark a path through the area of policy by detailing the simplest known ways to perform essential actions. Billing procedures, payroll procedures, and hundreds of others form the body of rules that guide a company's routine operations. These are all subject to constant review and change.

Organizing

We organize for only one purpose, and that is to develop and carry out our plans to reach our agreed-upon objectives. In planning our organization, therefore, we must be goal- or objective-oriented, not function-oriented. The emphasis should be on what tasks we must perform and who must perform them to enable us to arrive at the objectives.

We want to do no more of any activity than we

believe necessary. Every proposal must be examined for its contribution toward company objectives; and, if its contribution cannot be pinpointed, it should be set aside. Hard experience teaches that it is much easier to add an activity than to eliminate one.

One of the main purposes of planning and organizing is to avoid crisis as change occurs. Yet management often forgets to plan for the impact of change on personnel requirements and organization structure—even though change is as critical here as it is in the areas of facilities, products, and marketing. Planning and organizing are so closely allied that they should never be separated; both are basic responsibilities of every manager.

People often have the idea that the most effective organization unit is a single individual, but this is not so. In the modern corporation a well-organized team of competent persons who are specialists in their areas can surpass the performance of an individual. The more capable and experienced the manager, the greater the team's opportunity for achievement. Frequently the beginning manager makes the mistake of thinking that he should know more about his area of responsibility than anyone who reports to him. The mature manager understands that this is impossible and that his success depends largely on the abilities of his subordinates. He chooses the very best people he can get and tries to involve them in the total management processes of his area, as we did at YAC by introducing the unit president concept.

In speaking of organization, businessmen have a tendency to talk in terms of classical organization charts.

For best results, however, management should be able to think as creatively about organization as it does about product design and other matters that entail business innovation. A company's structure should not be prefitted to a traditional pattern simply because this is the easy way—nor should it be made different for the sake of being different. As Chapter 6 describes, it should be carefully tailored to the company's needs so that management is comfortable with it.

In order to think creatively in this area, the professional manager must be a student of organization, with a sound understanding of the difference between line and staff, centralization and decentralization of authority, and primary and secondary authority (these terms are defined in the glossary at the back of the book). He also needs to recognize that organization has two dimensions—formal and informal. The formal organization can and should be described in writing and outlined on a chart. The informal organization, although unwritten, can be a powerful aid to managers who understand its value in conveying information up and down the line (see the section on communications at the end of this chapter).

Above all, the professional manager understands that if he is to be a true leader, he must demonstrate an ability to follow a leader. This requires a spirit of cooperation and a sense of stewardship, for as a member of a team he must often subordinate his own opinions and even his personal gain for the good of the whole. If he is not willing to be a follower as well as a leader, he should not work in corporation management but go into business for himself. Cooperation is the essence of teamwork.

Controlling

Controls are not punitive; they are set up to provide management with early warnings that events are not conforming to plan. Obviously there is no control where there is no plan, since the essence of control is to review progress against the plan. "Control" is both a noun and a verb. As a noun it means a report, prepared in as simple a form as possible at the time when it is needed, that presents the vital few elements management needs to know. As a verb, control refers to the action that will be taken on the basis of this information. No matter how accurate, well prepared, and timely the control report is, it is wasted if management does not do something about it.

Control does not imply centralization of authority; it is most effective in a company where authority is decentralized. And, in fact, successful decentralization demands carefully developed controls of the fast-feedback type. Not only should they instantly tell the person responsible how he is doing, but they should also supply others, particularly at higher levels, with enough information so that they can move quickly when help is needed. The essence of control is to set objectives for each level in the organization, spell out each person's duties and responsibilities, decentralize authority, and review progress against the plan.

Dr. Joseph M. Juran [1] classifies controls and the need for them into two categories: the vital few and the trivial many. He suggests that in every company, and in every segment of a company, there are a few

[1] *Managerial Breakthrough: A New Concept of the Manager's Job* (New York: McGraw-Hill, 1964).

operations vital to its success which should be controlled more carefully and more frequently than the trivial many. He divides control information into three classes: (1) need to know, (2) helpful to know, and (3) curiosity to know. Obviously management can keep control procedures simple by concentrating on the first class. The second, information that is helpful, can be provided as needed and to the degree needed. Class 3 information is not furnished as a part of control, but it is stored where those who are curious can look it up. Dr. Juran states:

> We could do with a good deal more mastery of the managerial process than we now possess.
>
> As managers, we should like to be able to do with confidence many things we now do with apprehension. We would like to be able to:
>
> Launch our Breakthroughs with confidence that the great majority will reach the goals we set.
>
> Establish our Controls with confidence that they will take off our backs the great bulk of our burden of fire fighting.
>
> Design our organization of work so that the great majority of men will find, on the job itself, the challenges and satisfactions required by the human race.[2]

Motivating

When company presidents in the round tables of AMA's Presidents Association are asked to name their biggest problem, many place it in the area of motiva-

[2] Ibid., p. 369.

tion: "I can't get my people to feel as committed as I do." "Too many of our employees work by the book, without thinking about the end result." "The team spirit is missing." But a little discussion quickly turns up the point that people will not feel committed to an end result unless they have first been involved in deciding what is to be done and how to go about it. I am convinced that the salvation of any company that has grown beyond one-man rule is true decentralization and the involvement of its people in the management process.

Looking back over the relatively brief history of management, we see that little was understood until recently about the value of participative management. Men such as Dr. Alfred J. Marrow [3] of the Harwood Manufacturing Corporation and Dr. Warren G. Bennis,[4] provost of the State University of New York, have done much to explore this subject. Dr. Bennis traces the evolution of management's attitude toward people over the past four centuries, beginning with the concept that he calls "coercion and fear." In this stage the supervisor or overseer literally held the power of life and death over his charges, often slaves or serfs. Then came the step to the idea of "authority and obedience," under which the overseer's power was derived from the physical symbols of his office and from his ability to directly affect the well-being of those under his jurisdiction.

[3] See Alfred J. Marrow, *Making Management Human* (New York: McGraw-Hill, 1957); Alfred J. Marrow, David G. Bowers, and Stanley E. Seashore, *Management by Participation* (New York: Harper & Row, 1967).

[4] Warren G. Bennis, *Changing Organizations* (New York: McGraw-Hill, 1966).

The next phase, the first real breakthrough, was that of "collaboration and reason." This occurred when the manager realized that if he were to obtain more than minimal effort from his subordinates, he had to make them understand what was to be done and why.

Dr. Bennis terms the final stage "involvement and commitment." If people are to become truly involved in the management process—involved to the point where they make their best effort—they must participate in these processes deeply enough to feel responsible for the results.

It has been said from many platforms and in many books that involving everyone in the managerial process is not practical—that the decision-making power must be held by a few if a company is to move quickly and confidently in the entrepreneurial world. This is simply not true. It may be the easiest way to do things in the beginning, but it is not the most effective way. The operating details of the modern corporation are so complex, and technology changes with such rapidity, that top management finds it increasingly difficult to dictate decisions. No company can achieve its real potential unless all segments of the managerial hierarchy participate in management—and participate far more fully than most people think possible. Although it is overworked today, the word "revolution" is appropriate in this connection. Professional management, as it is practiced in Dr. Bennis's fourth and final stage, induces a controlled revolution in thought, challenge, and action.

Personal versus group objectives. Discussions about the feasibility of involving people in company objectives frequently emphasize the conflict between an employee's personal objectives and those of the firm. This approach is taken by Dr. Harry Levinson in a thought-provoking article, "Management by Whose Objectives?" In his conclusion he states:

> Management by objectives and performance appraisal processes, as typically practiced, is inherently self-defeating over the long run because it is based on a reward-punishment psychology that serves to intensify the pressure on the individual while really giving him a very limited choice of objectives. Such processes can be improved by examining the psychological assumptions underlying them, by extending them to include group appraisal and appraisal of superiors by subordinates, and by considering the personal goals of the individual first. . . .
>
> Not having to be continuously on the defensive and aware of the organization's genuine interest in having him meet his personal goals as well as the organization's goals, a manager would be freer to evaluate himself against what has to be done. Since he would have many additional frames of reference in both horizontal and vertical goal setting, he would need no longer to see himself under appraisal (attack, judgement) as an isolated individual against the system.[5]

Unquestionably an area may exist between the individual and the system where goals do not coincide, and the problems arising there require serious consideration. Yet I believe that we tend to overreact to the difficulty of relating a man's personal objectives to those

[5] Harry Levinson, "Management by Whose Objectives?" *Harvard Business Review*, Vol. 48, No. 4 (July–August 1970), p. 134.

of the group. Almost everyone includes among his personal goals the desires to achieve, to belong, to be recognized, to participate. His inclination, unless it is thwarted by poor management practices, is to expect his work group to furnish opportunities for satisfying these goals. My experience has been that employees focus most intensely on their personal objectives in a work situation where there are no sound group objectives.

At YAC the need did not arise for complicating our fairly simple appraisal program with systems of group appraisal and appraisal of superiors by subordinates, as Dr. Levinson recommends. His is a recommendation that I think can create more problems than it solves. It was not an impossible task to bridge the gap between the individual and the system, even though our 5,000 employees represented a cross section with many different personal goals. In education, they ranged from people with only a few years of grammar school to those with several doctoral degrees; in political attitudes, from sponsors of the far left to champions of the far right; in temperament, from people dedicated to serving others to those dedicated to having others serve them. Naturally they did not all respond with equal enthusiasm to the challenge of pulling the company up off its plateau. But no one dragged his feet; no one failed to do at least an acceptable job in his area. By the time we had successfully established a new organizational structure and new patterns, even employees who had shown the least interest at the beginning clearly took pride in the achievement.

Leadership. As Dr. Bennis says, "Effective leadership depends primarily on mediating between the individual and the organization in such a way that both can obtain maximum satisfaction." [6] A manager's ability to do so is directly related to the characteristics of leadership he possesses, but these are difficult to define. Certainly he cannot act as a leader by avoiding the role of decision maker; participative management is not group decision making. A group seldom arrives at a good decision; it seeks a compromise solution that all its members can accept, and compromises are never creative. In participative management the decision maker benefits from the contributions of everyone concerned so that he can come to a better decision than he could make on his own. And it is when all the participants have a clear image of the ultimate objective that the manager's decision maximizes their total experience, imagination, and creativity. His people acquire understanding of the objectives by having been involved in setting them, even though the final version may contain nothing that they personally contributed.

In an organization based on participative management, every manager must develop his own pattern of leadership. He might first consider the kind of leader he wants to be by listing the qualities that he himself likes in a leader. This exercise does not reveal the essential nature of leadership, however, for the Golden Rule in its literal sense is not universally applicable. No two people are alike, and even the same person sometimes differs from day to day. Rather than treating his associates as if they were copies of himself, the sensitive manager puts time and effort into understand-

[6] Bennis, op. cit., p. 66.

ing them as individuals. When he encounters unusual behavior, he is aware that it is not typical of the person, and he exercises restraint and compassion to help the man unlock the cause. He provides understanding and encouragement in the form needed at the time.

The higher a manager goes in an organization, the less effectively he can make operating decisions alone. The earlier he can involve his subordinates in active discussion of a situation, the greater the likelihood that they will introduce better ideas than he could work out by himself. He must develop a high degree of skill in asking the question that stimulates them to think more clearly and more broadly. And at all costs he must avoid the "It can't be any good if I didn't think of it" syndrome. The true leader shows strong evidence of his willingness to change when presented with a better suggestion. And, when he himself is making a suggestion or recommending a change, he does not confront his people with a detailed program to carry out. He presents his idea gradually until they grasp what he has in mind and begin to enlarge on it—and perhaps to improve it. In the process it becomes their idea, and they not only understand it thoroughly but become committed to it. At the YAC Corporation it happened that the ultimate organization structure arrived at by the group was virtually identical with one I had worked out and put in my desk drawer a year before. No one ever saw it; the new structure was theirs, not mine.

Communication. Of all the factors involved in the ability of people to live and work together, communication is perhaps the most difficult. Although one of the most important rules in the field of communications is to be a good listener, few of us ever develop the art of listening. We are preoccupied with our own work, ideas, and ambitions; and, even when we are quiet, we are busy thinking of our next remarks. Listening demands intense concentration on the words being spoken. Even more difficult, it requires an effort to determine what is behind the words. What is the speaker's real purpose? What is he actually trying to tell us? To discover this, we must know the person well—which returns us to the point that the manager must take time to understand his people, their ambitions, ideas, and ability to express themselves. Only then can he evaluate what is being said.

In the proper climate, communication often occurs spontaneously. The skillful manager does not leave it to chance, however; he makes it happen by setting up the mechanisms for communication. For example, he schedules regular meetings to explore important points. These meetings should not be free-form; they must be structured, with an agenda and a competent chairman who can keep the discussion on the track and draw conclusions wherever possible. If it is a decision-making session, the person responsible for the decision should be the chairman. In addition to meetings, the manager should establish methods for reporting vital information on a need-to-know basis. The reporting machinery should be as simple as possible while fulfilling its purpose of keeping people informed.

To encourage good communication in a company, management must support the principle that people have a right to know about anything which concerns them. They should feel that they need only raise a question in order to get an answer. The fact that they have this right is sometimes more important than the information itself.

Yet the manager must also recognize that there is a difference between total communication and telling people what they really want to know. Here again, he must take the time to discover the true purpose of a question and then answer it to the person's satisfaction. He should avoid replying with a flood of information that is often useless and may even be harmful if it is beyond the employee's ability to grasp.

One of the most valuable aspects of a company's informal organization is that the lines of communication are open between anyone who can provide useful information and anyone who wants it. Communication does not follow the chain of command—with one exception. When the information gathered leads to a recommended change in policy or plan, obviously the final decision must be made within the formal organization so that it does not violate the lines of accountability. The one danger in the right of free communication is that people may take advantage of it to circumvent their immediate superior. Everyone in the organization must be alert for questions that usurp supervisory rights or accountabilities; answers should not be given in such cases.

With this reservation, the right to communicate with anyone who can help him do his job better is the right of every employee. The channels and means of communication are very important to the successful development of the unit president concept. Management must give intensive thought not only to establishing the structure of communication and the forms of communications, both written and verbal, but also to making certain that it all takes place.

4

The Planning Cycle

PLANNING is the primary element of management which logically precedes all others, since without planning a manager would not have activities to organize, would not require people, would have no one to direct, and would have no need to control. While no manager can successfully accomplish his task unless he is proficient in all the elements, control is peculiarly dependent upon planning. This is because we organize to accomplish our plan, and control is a process of making certain that events conform to plan. Therefore no manager can control who has not planned. As we said earlier, planning is to a large extent the job of making things happen that would not otherwise occur. It is an intellectual process, the conscious determination of course of action.

Planning is not a forecast or a prediction; it is a

commitment. Long-range planning should be not an attempt to predict the future but a blueprint for changing a business from its present status to another status of our own choosing. A forecast is not a plan any more than a budget is a plan—both are important parts of the process, but in themselves they are not plans. Managers in many companies have the idea that, when they prepare a complete statistical budget, it constitutes their plan; this is not true. It becomes a plan only when the physical actions they are going to take to meet the targets established in the budget are outlined in detail. There must be a timetable for accomplishment of the actions and a true possibility of accomplishment. In addition, the needs for the people who are required to carry out the actions must be indicated and specific responsibilities designated.

Therefore planning really consists of three important elements: the fiscal and physical aspects and the organization and manpower. The fiscal aspects include the expense, income, cost, cash flow, and profit that the planner anticipates will be required and will result from the efforts expended. The physical plan concerns the things management is going to do to take it from where it is to where it wants to go. The organization and manpower plan is the structure and "people" needs for implementing and carrying out the plan as outlined. All three are essential, like the legs on a three-legged stool.

Where does the planning process take place? In my opinion, the only sound answer is that it takes place at every level of the organization. In the unit president concept it is essential that the president of the unit, whatever it is, be responsible for the planning function of his unit. His participation in the planning process will vary, however—a point that will be discussed in Chapter 5.

In our implementation of the unit president concept at the YAC Corporation, great care was taken to make certain that the objectives agreed upon with each president were truly those which he not only could influence but could be held accountable for achieving. For example, there is no use giving the president of the warehouse and shipping company in one of the manufacturing plants objectives that have to do with return on investment, penetration of the market, profit margins, and the like. His objectives should be in such areas as unit costs, labor turnover, shipping errors, shipping damage, and his budget. It is true that he must understand the relationship between his objectives and the objectives of the other elements of the organization; but he has the satisfaction of knowing that when he reaches his objectives, he has made his contribution toward the total objectives of the company.

Planning cannot be done solely by a central staff, nor can it be done solely by the unit president himself. He should be the leader in the planning process, but here again the involvement and commitment of his people are essential to its ultimate success. Staff must provide help and information, and they must provide a "plan for planning." But accountability for the actual planning belongs to the individual unit president and must never be diluted.

Since his personal involvement is required, the obvious question is where the unit president will find the time to do this planning—particularly since a plan is not cast in concrete but is subject to constant review and change as the realities differ from the assumptions. Again, the answer lies at least in part with the practice of the philosophy of management known as decentralization. If the unit president has truly delegated that which he can and should, he will have the time to meet the planning needs of his particular unit.

At the YAC Corporation the four questions we asked each unit president for his area of the business were as follows: (1) What must be done to safeguard the satisfactory results we are now achieving in our present operations? (2) What opportunities do we see for improvement in expansion of current operations, and what must be done to evaluate them or to make them possible? (3) What must be done to correct or overcome weaknesses in the present operations? (4) What must be done to thwart or reduce a threat that can be foreseen to future operations?

The Planning Process

At YAC we adopted the following questions as the basis of our planning process. When we had answered them satisfactorily, we believed that we had developed a sound process and a sound plan.

1. *Where are we? What business are we in?* To answer, we had to ask ourselves about our strengths and our weaknesses, our position in the market, our competitions, and our objectives. We had to make an unbiased and honest evaluation of every aspect of the operation

involved, whether it was the corporation as a whole or any unit of it. If these first questions are not answered honestly, management is laying an unsound foundation for the whole planning process.

2. *Where do we want to go?* Here we had to ask questions such as these: What business do we want to be in? How big should we be in the marketplace? What market penetration do we seek? Are we to be a national or international company? What profits do we want to achieve? What segment of the market do we want to serve?

3. *When do we want to achieve these objectives?* The answer involved drawing up a timetable for each step or action.

4. *What will we have to do to get from where we are to where we want to go?* All the necessary details were worked out to specify what actions would have to be taken and when they would have to be taken.

5. *Who will do what?* Every element of the plan together with the timetable for that element was assigned to someone in order to make sure that nothing would be overlooked, that there would be an accountable person, and that a definite time was established for accomplishment.

6. *What resources will it take?* This involved questions of money, manpower, facilities, and the like.

7. *Can we do it?* This is the vital question. In areas where we found that we could not, we went back and reviewed our objectives and plans to make them attainable, desirable, and acceptable.

At the YAC Corporation we already had a form of planning, as does everyone else. Some of it was in writing, some was formal, some was informal. That it was less than successful was recognized by all. Our objectives were largely short-term. As for the three types of planning discussed in Chapter 7, we did not have a strategic plan worthy of the name, and our operational planning was usually for the next year or even the next selling season. Insofar as conceptual planning is concerned, we had never heard of the term, let alone practiced it to any degree.

We quickly realized that if we were to begin growing again as a company, intensive thought and work would be needed in order to change the course that we had been traveling. We knew that it was one thing to stay on our plateau and quite another to move to higher grounds. We agreed that one of the purposes of planning as we envisioned it was to make a choice of alternatives and to channel the utilization of assets in such a manner as to gain the most from the efforts of people. Yet to move hastily into the area of formal planning without proper thought, proper understanding, and proper study would be not only unwise but even disastrous.

Introduction to Planning

To feel our way into the formal planning process at the YAC Corporation, we developed a beginning concept which took the form of an introduction to planning. This we used as the vehicle to bridge the gap between little or no planning in depth and the desired total planning process for the company. Our approach, which was admittedly rather primitive and has since been refined, took the following form.

To have each unit president learn from actual personal experience the value of planning, it was suggested that he list about five of the most pressing problems in his area of responsibility, as well as several opportunities for improvement—in cost reduction, sales, or whatever. The next step was to select two or three of the problems and opportunities for detailed study by him and his people. We asked them to write down as clearly as possible exactly what the problem or the opportunity was, and to list as many contributing factors as they could. They were to group similar problems or opportunities together for easier consideration. Next we asked them to list as many solutions as they could for each group and to analyze the solutions for their quality, cost, complexity, and relationships to solutions from other groups.

Finally, we suggested that they outline a plan for overcoming the problems or for taking advantage of the opportunity, listing (1) actions to be taken in sequence, (2) timing of the actions, (3) the person who would be responsible for each action, (4) the results anticipated, and (5) the time when the plan would be reviewed against results.

We felt that this approach would give the participants an opportunity to experience the process of planning in a simple way and to see the results that can be gained from the process. A second step, or even an alternative to the first approach, is to have the unit president—

1. List all the operational actions that are performed in his area of responsibility and evaluate the performance of each operation as either good or bad.
2. List all the developmental projects that he and his people have under consideration or under way and classify each as either an opportunity or an attempt to ward off a danger.
3. Group them into related families for the purpose of simplification.
4. Put them in the order of their importance.
5. Develop a provisional plan incorporating as many projects in both categories as can be successfully carried out during the planning period—say, a year. This plan should include—
   - A statement of the purpose or nature of the business or function.
   - A list of the objectives or results that are being sought.
   - A list of assumptions that are being made about general business conditions during the execution of the plan.
   - The specific actions that will be taken to achieve the objectives—the sequence and timing of each action and the person responsible for carrying it out.
   - The resources that will be required and when they will be available.
   - Provision for regular review sessions to compare actual results with the plan and to take corrective action where necessary.

47

As management approaches the end of this provisional planning period, it is now in a better position to develop a procedure for formal planning tailored to fit company needs. In the course of formulating the provisional plan, management has worked out the corporate strategic plan and business direction policies and is ready to institute formal operational planning in all areas of the business.

The provisional plan is obviously not complete, nor does it always cover every aspect of the business. Nevertheless, it is a step toward developing an understanding of what planning is, how it works, and what its benefits can be. It also gives management experience in the problems related to planning in the company, so that a more satisfactory formal planning process or plan can be developed.

At YAC we agreed in the early stages of learning to plan that the purpose of our planning was to protect that which we were doing well, to improve or correct that which was unsatisfactory, to make the most of our opportunities, and to head off the dangers that we faced or anticipated. This experience led us to the realization that planning does provide a systematic means by which a company can become what it wants to become.

Formal Plan for Planning

From the experience we gained in the introduction to planning phase and the provisional plan for planning, we all had grown to realize the importance and benefits of planning in our operations. We were ready to develop a formal "plan for planning" and make it a way of corporate life. All of us now had a clear idea of the purpose of planning, and we had achieved the commitment of top management support and time, which are essential for its success. We agreed that we were going to spend not only time but money on it. For one thing, we would provide experienced talent at a staff level to coach and advise the unit presidents. The planning coordinator would report to the chief executive officer, in this way insuring the chief's support and participation. We would also spend money to obtain the soundest data that could be made available in order to base our plans on hard facts.

Perhaps more than any other process, planning represents the condition in which the upper levels of management establish objectives that then flow throughout the entire organization. The corporate objectives become the focal point for the total planning process, with each segment of the company preparing its supporting plan. Top management does not know the feasibility of its overall objectives until every segment reports its plan and these are totaled. Thus the planning process begins at the very top, flows through the organization, and returns to the top (see Exhibit 4-1). Only then is it known whether or not the original objectives are obtainable, acceptable, and desirable.

Since all parts of the company were involved, we wanted to keep the plan for planning as well as the plan itself as simple as possible. We wanted them both to be concise and easy to read. Also, we wanted to record them in such a manner that they were easy to alter,

Exhibit 4-1. Pyramid of planning.

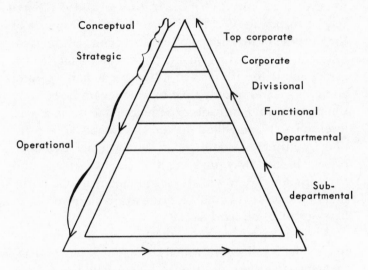

because plans are living documents that are subject to change as realities differ from the assumptions.

We agreed that the cycle of planning begins with the establishment of objectives. Next comes the determination of assumptions about general business conditions —the state of the economy, competition, and the like. The plan is developed on the basis of these assumptions, with actions designated that should lead to the achievement of the objectives. As the actual events take shape, they are compared with the plan. It is at this point that control is essential, since it provides a fast warning to change course. When it does, management reviews objectives, develops new assumptions, forms a new plan, and watches the emergence of new realities. As shown in Exhibit 4-2, this is a continuous cycle, and the plan must therefore be developed to allow for flexibility.

We recognized that if our plan was to be complete, every element of management and every responsibility had to be included. We considered that the seven elements of planning referred to all levels of the organization, not merely to the top. Each unit president had to answer the seven questions; his objectives plus all the objectives of the other unit presidents equaled the corporate objectives. In his own area of responsibility, we asked him to define the services he offered and the purpose of these services in the corporate scheme. For example, if his area involved the market, he was to give detailed answers to questions about its nature and characteristics, its trends, the company's share of it and competitive position, the competitive products and services, the nature and forms of distribution, customer-usage trends, and the price-demand relationship. The unit president was then to analyze the strengths and weaknesses of each segment of his operation.

One of our problems at YAC was that we were more engineering-oriented than marketing-oriented. To provide the means to lift us from our plateau, we decided that we had to become more sophisticated in the marketplace. A complete reexamination of our ways of going

Exhibit 4-2. Planning cycle.

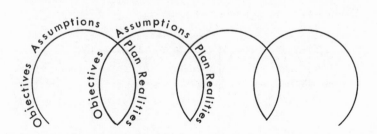

to market resulted in drastic changes to enable us to achieve our fair share of it. Further, we agreed that in all elements of the business our purpose was to serve the customer; whatever function we were in, we had to support the marketing effort. Accordingly, our total formal planning began with marketing. As Arthur "Red" Motley, president of Parade Publications, puts it, "Nothing happens until somebody sells something." Each division had to develop its own marketing plan of action and establish its objectives in the marketplace. Plans for all technical functions, facilities, manufacturing, finance, personnel, and other elements of a division were to support the marketing plan. When summarized and consolidated, these would become the divisional long-range plan. All the divisional plans plus the corporation's acquisition program and the plans for corporate finance, administrative services, and personnel needs would equal the overall corporate plan (see Exhibit 4-3).

Assumptions About General Business Conditions

We have learned by experience over the years that we must spend more time and thought on developing

Exhibit 4-3. Market-oriented planning.

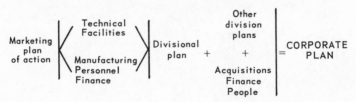

assumptions as to what the future may be like. We need not only to improve the quality of the assumptions themselves, but also to make certain that we include the factors which have the greatest impact on the business. Each assumption, too, must be analyzed to determine whether it is a limiting factor or an opportunity.

Here are some of the factors that almost all companies should include in their list of assumptions: gross national product, population trends, growth of the economy, shifting age brackets, the rate of inflation that can be expected, sociological pressures and changes, legislative actions (federal, state, and local), changes in technology (not only those that directly affect the business but those that are indirect, including changes that affect ecology), attitudes and trends in government thinking, military demands upon the economy, the international economy (imports, exports, inflation, and the like), the political climate, the labor situation (within the company, within the industry, and in industry as a whole), the financial climate (the supply of money, cost of money, and financing likely to be obtainable), availability of the workforce (including all types of labor needed, not only for shop operations but for management), rates of unemployment, the impact of automation, and shifts in the policy, nature, and quantity of competition.

Market Potentials and Opportunities

A company that is truly to be prepared for tomorrow's markets must be close to its customers and knowledgeable about their needs, both recognized and unrecognized. The story of industry is filled with cases in which products and services were taken to the customer that he had not requested but found that he did in fact need. Such cases arise from a careful study of the market combined with the use of the company's technology and experience in developing products and services. Capitalizing on market potentials involves three areas: (1) market opportunity or needs, (2) products, and (3) technology. Any combination of these might provide the breakthrough or improvement that the company is seeking.

In studying market opportunities, management must look not only at the present market but at the future one, at the latent as well as the unknown or unforeseeable market. In studying products, it should measure the present products against the market needs in order to improve what it offers to the customer. The same type of analysis should be applied to new products that are in the works or the plans and unknown products that are nothing more than a specification and perhaps at the moment cannot be produced. The study of technology follows the same pattern as that of products and includes the known technologies, the improved technologies that are being worked out, new technologies that management recognizes a need for and seeks to develop, and unknown technologies which would be in the nature of a breakthrough. If these areas are carefully and thoughtfully studied in terms of their multiple interrelationships, management is in a position to develop an effective marketing plan.

Where Do We Want to Go?

In determining where we want our company to go over the period of time of the plan, we set objectives which are preliminary or tentative in the sense that until all the plans are worked out, we cannot be certain that they are attainable or even desirable. Some of the questions that have to be carefully answered in setting these objectives have to do with the purpose of the business. They are different from the question of what business we want to be in; they could be stated as follows: Why are we in business? What service do we wish to render? What is our total overall objective?

Financial objectives concern growth or gross sales, profitability, margin, return on investment, earnings per share, and any other such criteria that may be useful in a particular enterprise. Besides these, management should decide on general criteria for the business it wants to be in: the nature of the business (civilian, military, domestic, international, consumer service, industrial, or whatever) and what share of the market it desires. (Some of these statements will be included in Chapter 5's discussion of conceptual planning.) In addition, limiting policies must be established. Ownership may be a limiting policy: Will we go public or not? Other policies may center on these questions: What degree of risk are we willing to take? What form of product distribution do we want? What about our people needs? Will we go international? Regional? National?

Management must also decide whether or not to

grow by acquisition as well as internally. If it does choose the acquisition route, what limitations will it place on external growth? Is management willing to give up absolute control of the business? Is it willing to diversify in nonrelated fields, or should it stick to fields that are fairly well related to the present types of business? What ratio should be established for internal versus external growth? Determining what business to be in might require a plural answer in a diversified company; management may be in several businesses.

The planning gap. In discussing where we want to go to establish our objectives, we must determine to the best of our ability what our growth would be if we confined ourselves to our present lines of business and

Exhibit 4-4. Development of planning gap.

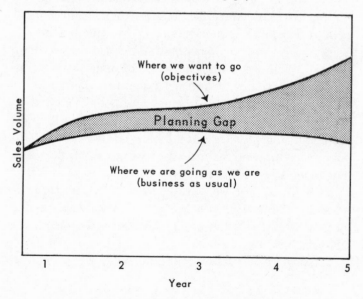

present markets. We plot this growth over the period of time indicated in Exhibit 4-4 and then plot a curve representing where we want to go according to our overall long-term objectives. The difference between the two curves represents the planning gap, which must be closed by new products, by acquisition, by new services, or by new facilities.

5

Conceptual, Strategic, and Operational Planning

TO shape its own future, maximizing opportunities, minimizing threats, and gaining the most from the efforts of its people, a company will be guided best when it has the three forms of planning shown in Exhibit 5-1. The conceptual plan is a long-range plan, the strategic plan covers the middle term, and the operational plan is a detailed, short-run blueprint for action. Together they sustain an integrated corporate effort for making the right things happen at the right time.

Conceptual Planning

As far as I know, conceptual planning in its modern form was developed by the Harris-Intertype Corporation in Cleveland, Ohio, under the leadership of George S. Dively, chairman of the board. This is the farthest-out planning that can possibly be done. Strategic planning, for example, may cover two to ten years, depending on the nature of the business and its cycles; conceptual planning may extend over ten to fifty years.

Exhibit 5-1. The three types of planning.

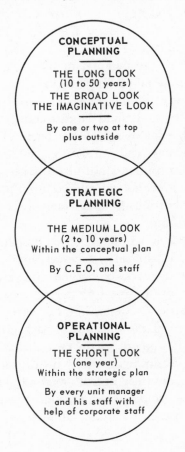

CONCEPTUAL
PLANNING
———
THE LONG LOOK
(10 to 50 years)
THE BROAD LOOK
THE IMAGINATIVE LOOK
———
By one or two at top
plus outside

STRATEGIC
PLANNING
———
THE MEDIUM LOOK
(2 to 10 years)
Within the conceptual plan
———
By C.E.O. and staff

OPERATIONAL
PLANNING
———
THE SHORT LOOK
(one year)
Within the strategic plan
———
By every unit manager
and his staff with
help of corporate staff

In conceptual planning, management takes a long view of just what it sees as the purpose of the business. At the Harris-Intertype Corporation the basic product lines were printing presses, and the firm served the printing industry. In the conceptual-planning analysis, Mr. Dively decided that the company should be in the business of communications—including oral, printed, illustrated, visual, wired, wireless, and code communications. The next step was to take a hard look at just what segment of this broad field should be the company's major thrust.

As shown in the pyramid of planning back in Exhibit 4-1, conceptual planning is limited to the very top of the company (in this case, Mr. Dively), since it is time-consuming and could be distracting to those who are responsible for operating the business from day to day. Mr. Dively used outside consultants—not only management consultants but also market research people, experts in technology, and research organizations— to help him outline the areas on which the company might concentrate.

This approach has been adopted in many other types of industries. In the early stages of their planning, for example, the managers of one farming group believed they were in the business of raising vegetables, citrus fruits, and cattle. On reflection, however, they decided that they were in the business of packaging fresh convenience foods. You can see the radical change this made in their total planning process: Now they were thinking more of the consumer and of methods for packaging vegetables that would reduce the amount of preparation at the point of use. It is quite a different approach from concentrating on techniques of harvesting vegetables and packing them almost directly from the fields. This type of thinking turned out to be so profitable that the managers made a further intensive study of what business they should be in and decided that it was the business of land utilization. Maximizing the land assets that they own does not preclude their continuing to provide fresh convenience foods, but it also opens up new opportunities. For example, they now ask themselves whether a particular piece of real estate should be used for vegetable farming, citrus growing, or cattle raising—or whether it should be devoted to real estate development, say, for home sites or recreation.

Similarly, this farming group decided that it was not in the subbusiness of cattle raising, but in that of preparing and processing meats for the end user. Consequently, it moved away from raising cattle and selling it on the hoof direct from the ranches to establishing its own feed lots. Eventually, it probably will go into meat processing. In the field of citrus growing, it is not simply raising oranges, lemons, and grapefruit; it is in the business of providing citrus juices and fresh fruit to the user in the most convenient form. The group has become involved in various ways of processing the fruit and in a total new marketing concept as well.

Another company that has benefited from this type of thinking is in the hotel and restaurant industry. The concept it has developed is that it is in the business of providing food, lodgings, and related services to the away-from-home public. This broader approach to the company's function could put it into the service station business, the travel agency business, the transportation business—into the business of providing services for people who wish to take a vacation or hold a meeting.

The conceptual plan thus pinpoints the areas that will receive the major thrust of the company as it grows into the total concept agreed upon. It should rank these areas in their order of importance or sequence. It must outline in sufficient detail the nature of the growth not only in markets and technology but also in facilities and people. And it must lay down the policies that will become guidelines or controls for the strategic plan. Obviously the conceptual plan provides a basis for strategic planning, which in turn is the basis for the operational or short-term plans.

Strategic Planning

In developing a strategic plan within the framework of the conceptual plan, provided the company has one, management must review all existing corporate policies. Additional policies may be needed and present policies may have to be changed in accordance with new thinking about the company's purpose. External policies that must be examined cover acquisitions, divestments, and the like; internal policies cover such areas as research and development, marketing, and finance.

Strategic plans usually extend over two to five years, though they sometimes cover as many as ten. Obviously the further a plan reaches into the future, the less specific its detail. To fill in the detail, strategic planning should be reviewed at least once a year (operational planning, in turn, should be reviewed twice a year).

Strategic planning involves the top echelons of the company. The chief executive officer naturally will be heavily involved, as will members of his service staff. There has been much controversy about the best way to organize for this type of planning. In a diversified company with divisions, my experience has been that the corporate strategic plan should be developed without the divisional vice-presidents or the group vice-presidents there. These men have great difficulty in divorcing themselves from the areas of their particular interests.

In turn, each group vice-president or division general manager can work with his people to develop his own strategic plan within the perimeters laid down by the corporate strategic plan. Reconciliation meetings can then be held in which the various divisional plans are fitted into the corporate plan and adjustments are made as needed. In my experience this has produced the best results, though there are managers who do not agree with me. Here again, management must tailor its procedure and even its plan for planning to fit the company's needs. Whatever method works best for you is the method you should have.

In the following discussion of strategic planning I am indebted to Don Trice, coordinator for planning of the Marriott Corporation, who is one of the most thoughtful men in this field.

Corporate-level strategic planning studies should first establish basic corporate business criteria. For example: "We will operate businesses in which we have an expertise that other companies do not have or in which we excel and can maintain a performance advantage.

We will analyze our strengths, build upon them, and concentrate on maintaining a competitive edge over our competition."

The planners then analyze and list the present areas of expertise or strengths relative to the competition. Such factors should be considered as quality of management, products or services, quality image, financing, location of facilities, training and manpower development, attitude of employees, and known and defined standards. Next it is well to list potential areas of expertise or strength that may not exist now.

You should decide what market you will serve. Are you going to produce a quality product? Will you maintain a pricing structure necessary to support this method of operation? Are you willing to offer a substandard, lower-cost product to meet competitive pricing? Or will you decide not to endanger the image that you want for your company? What are the minimum profit, sales, and return on investment criteria that you want to establish for each unit or division? On what basis will you set up criteria for all future expansion of the existing businesses? What criteria will you establish for new business types? Will you make these criteria lower, higher, or just equal to the minimum financial objectives of the company as it now exists?

Financial Objectives

Objectives in the financial area should be established in a pattern similar to the one previously outlined. Following are some representative questions.

Sales growth. What corporate sales growth do you expect? Will you state your objectives in real terms, that is, in base-year dollars or in units of product sold? Or will you include inflation? In setting these criteria, what percentage of annual consolidated sales growth do you desire as a minimum? What would be the median point of your sales growth? And what would be the maximum or upper limit within the present business? (Keep in mind that major acquisitions may exceed the upper limit, provided that this can be done without harming or diluting the existing business.) Is this sales growth that you desire over the period of the strategic plan to be an average, or is it to be steady growth rate with no wide fluctuations? What is the ultimate size of the market that you believe would be not only your fair share but also the maximum share that you can obtain without coming under government scrutiny?

Acquisitions. Do you want to be a conglomerate? Or would you rather confine the scope of your business to related businesses and services in which you have some expertise?

Corporate profit growth. What percent of net profit after taxes on sales do you consider the minimum acceptable? Do you wish to have the same percentage growth in profits that you do in sales? It is questionable whether you should establish an upper limit to profit growth. This may be desirable, however, since if profit proves to be excessive you may be holding an umbrella over current or potential competition and thus inviting new firms into the industry.

Leverage. Will you use the maximum amount of

debt? Will you keep equity at a minimum? If so, what ratio do you consider to be desirable? What is the spread of this ratio? Do you wish to confine use of equity to acquisitions only, financing all internal growth from internal sources, borrowed money, and the like?

Return on investment. This is an important measure of a project's worth, but it is not the only measure. Current interest rates must be taken into consideration. Will you retain all earnings in the company? If not, what percent are you willing to pay out in dividends? Will you establish a policy that return on investment must equal the corporate objective for rate of growth? To keep a healthy interest in the equity side of the business, what percentage of growth will be financed by the corporate return on investment?

Working capital. What is the minimum working capital that you believe desirable? At what point in the fiscal year will you measure how you are meeting this objective? What type of loan restrictions will you accept in your financing practices? What use will you make of short- and long-term loans? Will you establish a policy, for example, that short-term money may never be applied to long-term purposes? Will you define what use should be made of short-term money?

Reserve funds. What will be your policy and objectives in establishing reserves? Should you set up reserves for special opportunities and emergencies? What dollar amount of reserve funds should you have at some designated point during the fiscal year?

Common stock. What is your objective for the price range of your stock? At what point in its stock-market value per share would you consider splitting? What is the minimum value you would want for your stock in the market after it is split?

Principal stockholders. Do you want to encourage fund ownership in your stock? Do you want to encourage employee ownership? If so, by what devices? What are the minimum and maximum amounts of stock that you would want held by outsiders, by a member of management, or by a group of management people, should you be in a position to influence such policy?

Long-term financing sources. To whom will you look for long-term money? What type of security are you willing to offer? Would you mortgage property? How about sale and leaseback or leases themselves, as a form of long-term financing?

Investment opportunities. Will you set a priority on those that yield the greatest return on investment? On those that give you a more balanced position in the marketplace? What minimum returns do you want for any investment? What formula will you use for calculating return on investment? What will you dispose of in the event that capital is exhausted and the debt-equity ratio is seriously exceeded? What actions will you specify for your financial planning if such a situation appears possible?

Market Objectives

After defining the total scope of the business, management must decide what basic markets to serve within that area and how intensively to concentrate on each. Will they be local or domestic markets, international markets, consumer markets, industrial or corporate markets? What limitations should be placed at present on management's consideration of markets to serve? Specific questions for study might include the following.

What is your present position in each market that you now serve? What position do you want to achieve year by year throughout the period of the strategic plan? What maximum market penetration point will you establish? What rate of growth can you expect from your normal business-as-usual markets? Will this meet your growth objectives? If not, what are you going to do about it? What additional markets would you be willing to enter? What will you do about competition in the marketplace? Will you cut prices? Will you make special deals? Or will you hold to your pattern? If not, what conditions must exist before you change?

What is the future direction of your marketing efforts? Do you want to concentrate on your current business types in the geographical areas you now serve that in your opinion will yield the maximum profit? Or do you want to diversify? If you do, is it purely for the sake of diversification? If not, what areas of the markets you are considering are least vulnerable to decreases in profit margins? What ratio, for example, between labor dollar and sales dollar do you think desirable? Do you want to get into labor-intensive businesses, or to avoid them? How about capital-intensive businesses? If you select this type, what return would you expect, in keeping with the financial objectives that you have established?

At what point will you consider spinning off areas of business which show a declining profit or a failure to grow? What are the minimum criteria that you will permit in this situation? How long a period will you grant for trying to take corrective action? And since it is essential for control in strategic planning to monitor trends, what procedures or what staff groups will you establish to keep a close watch on changes in the market?

Group charters. The scope of the business assigned to each group or division must also be specified. Each group should be given responsibility for a particular market. Top management must be sure that all phases of the markets included in the scope of the corporation's pattern are properly covered, with a minimum of overlap. Once this is done, other market responsibilities can be assigned to the group or division—for example, market research, establishment of new businesses, adjustment of existing businesses, and elimination of outdated businesses as the needs of the market change.

Organization

As mentioned earlier, a plan should have three phases: its physical and fiscal aspects plus organization and manpower. Just as careful thought must be given to the organization-manpower aspects of the strategic plan as to the others. What is the structure that you believe will be required over the next, say, five years of the strategic plan? How many people of what kinds are you going to need that you do not now have? Where can you get them? When will you want them? What changes in reporting relationships will evolve as your company grows? Thus manpower planning, which will be discussed in detail in Chapter 6, is an essential part of the study of organization.

Major Corporate Strengths and Weaknesses

For the corporate strategic plan, the strengths and weaknesses of the company as a whole and of the corporate staff and divisions must be listed objectively and without reservation. These involve questions about the firm's position in the industry, its ability to provide funds, its image and reputation with all the groups it affects, and its management practices.

Is yours truly a professionally managed company? Are key executives tied down by day-to-day operational matters so that they have no time for careful planning and coordinating? How well do you plan? How good are communications among the various groups of the company? What type of control information is available? How effective is the research and development function? Are there losses due to labor turnover? Is the management development program adequate? These are representative areas that must be examined in evaluating strengths and weaknesses.

Major Corporate Threats

To take a hard look at the threats which may lie ahead, management must ask other questions—for example, about mergers, about technological change, about the money markets, and about such operating costs as construction, labor, and land.

What new companies may be coming into the industry and bringing large capital resources? What about the patterns of violence in the country today? Are you particularly subject to subversive actions by a militant group? How vulnerable are you to governmental controls? What is the attitude of government agencies toward your particular industry?

Do you face increases in labor and materials costs which may outpace your ability to raise prices? Are you in danger of securing too large a share of a market from the antitrust standpoint or from the standpoint of vulnerability to obsolescence? Are you too small in the market to be effective? These are some of the threats to be considered when preparing the strategic plan.

YAC Corporation's Strategic Plan

At YAC we held many discussion meetings on the need for establishing a corporate strategic plan in order to get the company moving again. Following is a summary of the objectives and the approach to planning that we worked out.

I. A strategic plan includes these essentials.
   A. It clearly states the basic company purpose: What business or businesses are we in, and what areas of each are we in? What business or businesses should we be in, and to what degree?
   B. It provides a carefully selected strategy to accomplish this purpose—to achieve the position in each business that we believe desirable.
   C. It describes not only the goals of the strategy but also the means for monitoring progress toward them.
   D. It specifies the conditions and environment both inside and outside the company—in each of our businesses—which will permit the firm to attain its goals.

    E. It defines the best allocation of resources between the near-term purpose of efficiency and the long-term purpose of continuity and improvement (research versus cost reduction, for example).

    F. It identifies the key decisions that must be made to integrate current operations, new developments, and acquisitions into the company's longest-range plans.

II. Strategic questions.

    A. What businesses are we in? What segment of each do we serve? How big are they, and what percent of the market do we represent? What is our acceptance by customers? What is their image of us? What are the trends in each business—sales, products, prices, uses? What is our profit trend?

    B. What areas closely related to our businesses are logical directions for expansion on the basis, principally, of our current know-how, facilities, and marketing practices?

    C. What closely related areas are possibilities for expansion except that we don't have the required know-how, facilities, and marketing practices?

    D. What are our management capabilities? This requires a management audit and inventory at all levels, basically to determine the following for each man: how he is performing on his present job, what his strengths and weaknesses are, what can be done to make him more effective, what his potential is, when he will realize it, and what help he needs to realize it.

    E. What are our resources in technological skills at all levels?

    F. What are our facility and financial resources and capabilities? What financial leverage do we have?

III. Fundamental strategic policy.

    A. Divestment, merger, acquisition: Each element of the business and each type of business should be carefully examined in the light of findings from I and II. Decisions must be made as to whether these elements should be spun off in some manner or used as a basis for merger or acquisition. Whether or not to dispose of the company as a whole must also be considered. If this were the decision, however, it would more likely be accomplished division by division than as a whole.

    B. Diversification by internal development: Each element of the business must be examined on the basis of findings from I and II to determine possibilities for internal development.

IV. Diversification planning.

    A. The first question to be asked is do we want to grow? If so, how much, over what period of time?

    B. How much will occur if we continue as we are? How much will occur if we follow a policy of divestment, merger, and acquisition (see IIIA)?

    C. We must decide on basic policies such as whether we will be a holding company or an operating company, whether we will aim for vertical integration or horizontal integration, what markets we will serve and how we will serve them, how far we will expand geographically, how hard we will push development within the company, how deeply we will go into acquisition, and what small operations we will make larger and more viable. If such decisions are not made, and we have no firm policy as to the nature of our businesses, we have no way to evaluate ideas and possibilities as they present themselves. We tend to waste time considering them all, and we may be led into acquiring dissociated businesses that force us into a holding-company setup.

D. We must examine, classify, and eliminate diversification possibilities to come up with a minimum number (two or three areas at most) on which to concentrate.

E. We must decide what degree of risk we can afford to take: How much can we afford to lose?

F. We should fix a rate of growth that would be challenging and then try to achieve it in an orderly manner year by year, always watching closely to see if the planned actions are bringing the predicted results.

G. We must be ready and willing to cut out a project that is not making it—there should be no false pride.

H. We must recognize that there will be failures and prepare for them even though we do everything possible to avoid them.

I. We must set our growth rate in numbers—these are our targets. Can we do it with our present management? With our present financing? Probably not. How can we get price-times-earnings up? After we set objectives, we must analyze them to see if they are a physical and financial impossibility. If so, we must adjust them.

J. We must remember to protect the golden goose or geese; our diversification program should not be carried on at the expense of basic business.

K. We must assemble competent manpower to handle this type of program.

L. Operating management can and will make suggestions, but it must receive guidance from top management based on criteria approved by the board of directors.

M. Once the growth rate is set, it should be changed only reluctantly, and the change should be made only by top management.

N. The first step should be to make assumptions about the risk involved, both in the total effort and in each proposal.

O. The second step is to make assumptions about results and actions.

    1. Environmental assumptions: Should we limit ourselves to the United States? Or should only the majority of our business be in this country? Where else might we operate businesses? In answering, we should give reasons that are as specific as possible. We must examine all areas— political, economic, financial, and manpower— and in making changes in our original assumptions we should base them on facts, not emotions.

    2. Assumptions about what businesses we want to be in.

        a. Our criteria might be that we receive an ROI at least equal to what we now have and that the business be compatible with our capabilities and technical know-how.

        b. If a business looks good to us, we should ask ourselves what we have to offer it. What do we know about it? What unique characteristics do we have which lead us to believe we can make a real contribution to that business?

        c. We should recognize that we are taking a risk when we expect to buttress one of our weaknesses through diversification. It is safer to see what strengths we can offer the other business.

d. For internal development, we should look from within outward so that we keep to areas we know and understand.

e. Our acquisitions may not be directly connected, but it is best if they are in the same environment and offer an opportunity to broaden our base in that environment.

f. It is usually more desirable to acquire several small- to medium-size companies rather than one large one; they are easier to absorb. If they are too small, however, they can be a nuisance.

g. Whatever the target is, usually we must come up with two or three times that in possibilities.

h. When a proposition passes the first screening, it should go to the executive committee of the board for quick action. If it is approved for further study, the quality of the study is paramount.

i. It is usually best to have one man responsible for seeing the proposition through. After the first careful study, fast reevaluations can be made at various stages.

j. One way to organize this effort is to set up a top management strategy board that meets once a month. Usually it can make an immediate decision on whether or not to proceed. The board of directors makes the final decision, but this group starts the chain and appoints one man to coordinate it. A group in the company is selected to make evaluations in addition to their regular duties. This task-force assignment gives them a feeling of entre-preneurship and involvement. Anyone in the company can present an idea to the strategy board, but he must develop it into a proposition beforehand. To do this he usually needs the help of others, but his effort proves that he is interested. Thus people and money are required to back up diversification planning. The top strategy group acts as a review board and receives reports on progress, and in evaluating propositions it must consider all limiting policies (such as antitrust).

V. Division planning.
  A. Our divisions should list all their operations and evaluate them.
  B. They should list each project and specify whether its purpose is to cash in on an opportunity or block a threat.
  C. These projects should be organized into related groups and rated in order of importance.
  D. The divisions must develop specific plans to retain what is good, overcome what is bad, and cash in on as many opportunities, taken in order of importance, as is practical.
  E. A division's management should look at the business of the division as if it were their own. The managers should decide what they would do with it to reduce costs and to make it grow and become more profitable. Then they should consider what other uses, both closely related and more remote, they can see for their know-how and capabilities.
  F. A manpower audit is an essential part of divisional planning (see IID).

77

G. Consolidation of research and operations should be studied to reduce costs and maximize the company's know-how and facilities (for example, to reduce the number of locations).

H. A critical review of research and development expenditures and results over the past five years should reveal how sharp our programs really are.

I. In unsuccessful operations, study successful competitors. What do they do that we don't? Come up with a plan to get the operation firmly in the black —in one year, for example.

Here are some of our conclusions at the YAC Corporation after all these studies were made. We definitely decided that we would not grow by acquisition. Our team looked at many companies whose product lines would fit in with ours, but in each case we concluded that the problems of acquiring and integrating were greater than those we would face if we went ahead on our own.

In these studies we learned much about the product lines of the possible acquisitions, so the time and effort were not wasted. Another secondary benefit was to encourage us to look inward for our own salvation—to realize that the acquisition route was a short-term glory road. At least we knew what our problems were, but we did not really know what the acquired company's problems would be. We also concluded that if a business was available for acquisition, it must have problems, and that we would have to become adept at discovering the problems if we were to cope with them. And the big question of what we could add to the acquired company was never satisfactorily answered within our own group. So we resisted the temptation of acquiring, to our subsequent gratification.

Since we had decided that our "acres of diamonds" were in our own backyard, our best opportunity was to maximize our know-how in the businesses we were in. We divided the company into divisions based primarily on the way the products were taken to market, although the manufacturing facilities were also separated.

As mentioned earlier, we were heavily oriented toward engineering and manufacturing. We had neglected the marketing aspects of the business, particularly marketing of the product lines with the greatest growth. These were mass-produced, designer-styled products which went to retailers through a distributor organization and then to the consumer. We did not have a strong distributor organization; it was highly technical but was not geared to mass merchandising. Nevertheless, it contained some loyal and competent people, with whom we decided to work through an expanded market research and market analysis group. We established quotas by product lines for each distributor and his territory. Then we developed with him an organization plan and a financial plan that would enable him to meet the quotas. We set up a timetable for accomplishment, with progress points designated along the way, that would eventually give us the total share of the market which we had to have if we were to achieve our corporate objectives.

The result was that in many cases we took over the franchises and developed factory branches. We had come to the conclusion that we were really financing the distributors anyway, yet they were individual entrepreneurs whose needs and objectives were frequently quite different from our own. We had also found that the required know-how was usually not available in a distributor organization, and we were forced to supply it with our own staff. Furthermore, service was particularly important in this business, and many times a distributor was not able or willing to provide the kind of service that the customer demanded. Although we established factory branches in place of the distributor, we retained him in other phases of the business where he was in a better position to meet our needs.

We also broadened our product lines, and we added closely related lines that we first considered from an acquisition standpoint and then decided to develop on our own or have privately branded by other manufacturers. I believe this course brought us along faster than we could have come otherwise. If we had acquired truly successful manufacturers in the lines that we wished to branch into, they would in reality have acquired us. This would not have been acceptable, since one of our objectives was to retain control of our company.

To effect these changes we brought in some specially skilled and knowledgeable people, particularly in the middle and upper middle levels of our marketing management. We also hired one top-flight marketing man with a fine reputation and proven ability in the field. In the whole of our reorganization, he was the only top-level man brought in from the outside; we made it the rest of the way with the people we had. This was one of our great satisfactions, since it proved that sound management practices can enable people to develop to their greatest potential.

Operational Planning

Operating plans are based on the strategic plan and consist of short-term (usually one-year), step-by-step programs to take us where we want to go. Both the company as a whole and its parts should establish short-term objectives—financial as well as organizational—in which particular duties are allocated to each individual. The purpose is to have a definitive schedule that uses quantitative terms wherever possible.

The questions that should be asked in formulating operating plans are similar to those asked in strategic planning, except that they are more specific and detailed:

1. What is the purpose of the function (manufacturing, marketing, finance, and so on)? This question is not so easy to answer as might appear, but it must be considered in detail.

2. What is the environment in which the function operates—its climate, problems, limitations, opportunities?

3. What are the capabilities of the organization and the facilities?

4. What are the general assumptions on which planning will be based—for example, assumptions about strikes, labor shortages, materials shortages, and percent of inflation?

5. What market potential will be sought during this short term in order to meet the objectives?

6. What are the objectives themselves? For each function? For each of its elements?

81

7. What is the organization available? What are its strengths and weaknesses? Is it properly structured to do the job? What additional people will be needed?

8. What policies and procedures exist? Are they adequate? Can they be improved? What additional ones are needed?

9. What programs and projects will have to be instituted in order to reach the objectives?

10. What priorities and schedules will be established so that the plan can be carried out in an orderly manner?

11. What resources will be required—money, manpower, materials, facilities, and the like?

Like other types of planning, establishing operational plans begins with a marketing plan and a market forecast. The projects, programs, systems, and services that will be required to carry out the marketing plan must be spelled out in detail. Then each functional element in the organization must develop its own plan aimed at realizing its share of the projects, programs, systems, and services—marketing, production, technological, financial, personnel, and so on. The completion of the market forecast with all the expense—income ratios permits the development of a total projected P&L for that particular operation (see Exhibit 5-2). To prepare each functional plan, the total operation must be broken down into individual components, usually headed by a unit president. He must then work out his supporting plan for the total effort in order to meet the division's objectives. His plan should include his budget, his labor and materials needs, the necessary facilities and equipment, and everything else that he requires, expressed in quantitative terms wherever possible. Here again, a timetable should be established for each action, and responsibility for each should be assigned to a specific individual.

When completed, the operational plans are evaluated in terms of the divisional objectives, resources, and timing. Then the divisional plans are integrated and consolidated to make up the corporate operational plan,

Exhibit 5-2. Operational plans.

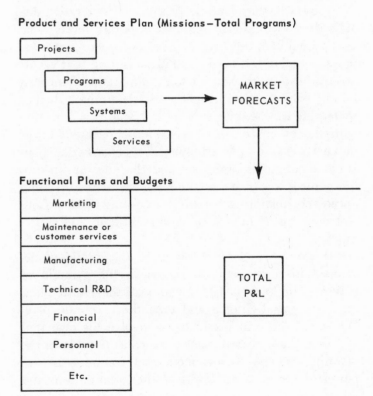

Product and Services Plan (Missions—Total Programs)

Projects

Programs

Systems

Services

MARKET FORECASTS

Functional Plans and Budgets

| Marketing |
| Maintenance or customer services |
| Manufacturing |
| Technical R&D |
| Financial |
| Personnel |
| Etc. |

TOTAL P&L

which is compared with the corporate objectives, re-sources, and timing. The overall evaluation of the plan results in a decision to go ahead with it or to reallocate effort or resources and formulate a different plan. The planners should be on the alert for alternative courses of action, and they must remember that everything may not work out exactly as indicated. While applying a dis-count factor for failure to achieve every goal, they should try to evaluate the degree of risk in each part of the plan.

Above all, the planning process is a reiterative one at both the divisional and the corporate levels. The operational plan must be reviewed every six months (or more frequently, if needed) to make certain that events are conforming to plan. If some important element is falling behind, management must determine whether something can be done quickly to bring it back in line with the others, or whether the other elements must be cut back too. For example, if the marketing plan is not meeting its objectives and the sales group can-not remedy the situation, there is no sense in going ahead and turning out products according to plan. Con-trol must be sensitive, evaluation constant, and action quick.

At the YAC Corporation each unit president de-veloped his own plan. As shown in the pyramid of planning in Exhibit 4-1, the total of these unit plans made up the divisional and then the corporate plan. We urged the unit president to involve his own staff and even the hourly workers as much as possible in the planning process. Involvement and commitment are powerful forces at all levels of the organization, and together they form one of the best motivating tools available to the manager. Each unit president at YAC submitted so many demands, not only for money and resources to improve his operations, but also for the services of staff groups, that we had to establish strong priorities. This was a complete reversal from the situation before the company was reorganized, when the attitude was "Leave me alone and I'll get my job done." Under the unit president concept, employees did everything they could to improve their operations, just as if the company were their own.

Organization for Planning

Corporate planning is one of the basic responsibilities of the chief executive officer, and the plan for each unit of the organization is the responsibility of the unit president. In my opinion, all plans should be coordinated by a single person: the director or coordinator of planning. In many companies there is a separation between fiscal planning and organization and manpower planning, yet in reality it is difficult to distinguish between what it is we are going to do and who is going to do it. The best approach is to assign organization and manpower planning to the same person, who reports to the chief executive officer and whose subordinates report to the general managers of the divisions.

The planning staff do not do the planning; they only see that it is done. They assist, they coordinate, they gather and develop data, they do everything in their power to make planning a success in the company.

But the people responsible for the individual function must do their own planning; otherwise they will not feel a personal commitment to the plan.

The planning staff on both the corporate and the divisional levels should be minimal. In most organizations, one person and a secretary. There may be an additional specialist, and some companies have the market research group reporting to planning. I recommend that the planning function be kept very simple and that market research, for example, be a function of the marketing department. It is important, however, that the staff services be available throughout the organization. The planning process calls for the best information which can be made available.

The position description for the coordinator of planning at the corporate level might take the following pattern:

Position Description
Coordinator of Corporate Planning

Basic Function: To aid corporate and divisional executives in the development of short- and long-term planning for their areas of responsibility; to develop staff within each division to coordinate divisional planning; and to create methodology and controls for divisions and the corporation that will show how results compare with plans. This responsibility to include all phases of planning—fiscal, physical, and organization planning.

Scope: The assigned functional responsibilities of this position extend throughout the corporation.

86

Major Responsibilities:

1. Assists the chief executive officer in analyzing the company's strengths, weaknesses, and opportunities and in establishing goals for corporate growth, sales, profits, return on assets and investment, products, markets, and related considerations. Serves the divisional or functional managers in a similar manner.

2. Coordinates the planning activities of the operating divisions so that they can directly relate their objectives and strategies to those of the corporation.

3. Assists division vice-presidents and their staffs in preparing their plans and action programs.

4. Analyzes divisional plans to assure that they are well conceived, are adequate to meet the divisions' needs and goals, capitalize fully on the potential of the divisions, and avoid duplication of effort.

5. Establishes methodology to see that meaningful performance reports are developed in order to evaluate the progress of divisions against attainment of objectives as set forth in their plans.

6. Assists division heads and their staff in developing more incisive annual operating plans through the establishment of longer-range objectives, plans, and programs.

7. Integrates all division plans and develops the corporate master plan. Makes sure that all division plans are in accord with approved corporate long-range plans and objectives.

8. Keeps top management executives informed of political, technological, marketing, or economic developments that may affect the corporate plans and strategies.

9. Maintains historical and current information on the corporation and assists its divisions in gathering pertinent data for marketing and sales analysis, distribution, services,

facilities, research and development activities, competition, and industry developments.

10. Coordinates information from sources outside the company that is needed as a basis for planning and analysis.

Relationships:

1. Reports to the chief executive and is accountable to him for proper fulfillment of planning functions and responsibilities.

2. Works closely with the operating divisions, particularly with the division heads and their staffs. Although this relationship will be of a functional nature and will not involve direct authority over the divisions, the coordinator of corporate planning will be alert to all division needs and problems. He will take the initiative in offering assistance and in acting where required.

3. Maintains outside contacts so that he can be alert to any developments which may be of significance to the company. Establishes liaison with outside planning and research organizations.

6

Organization:
The Corporate Structure

IN the development of the unit president concept at the YAC Corporation it was perhaps in the field of organizing that we did our best work. Although we did a credible job in planning and a good one in establishing the type of controls that we needed, our major effort went into breaking away from one-man rule and setting up a decentralized organization. Since the definition of duties and responsibilities is vital in the unit president concept, we had not only to restructure the entire company as described in this chapter, but also to rewrite all position descriptions and supporting data along the lines discussed in Chapter 7.

At the time the study began, we were a functional organization, with all marketing under one head, all

Exhibit 6-1. Corporate structure comparison: functional versus divisional organization chart.

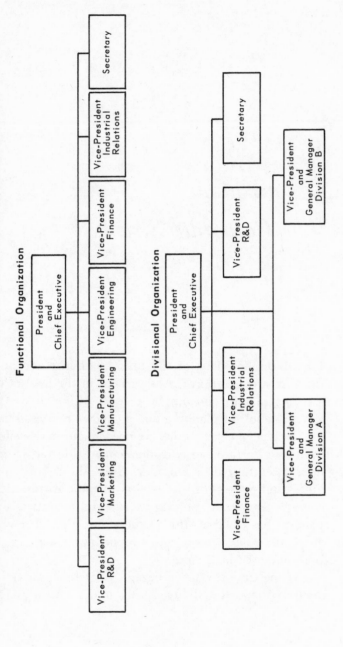

Functional Organization

President and Chief Executive

- Vice-President R&D
- Vice-President Marketing
- Vice-President Manufacturing
- Vice-President Engineering
- Vice-President Finance
- Vice-President Industrial Relations
- Secretary

Divisional Organization

President and Chief Executive

- Vice-President Finance
- Vice-President Industrial Relations
- Vice-President R&D
- Secretary
- Vice-President and General Manager Division A
- Vice-President and General Manager Division B

manufacturing under another, and so on. Yet we had two obviously different product lines. One, which went to market through distributors and dealers, was mass-produced and -styled. The other, a modular type of product which was produced in small lots and put together in different combinations, was usually sold direct to the consumer. From the design stage to the market-place these lines represented two entirely different problems, even though they were basically similar in technology, function, and purpose. We soon recognized that if we were going to get the company moving forward again, we had to reorganize it into at least two major divisions (see Exhibit 6-1). Actually there was a third as well—an international division which was partly self-contained and partly dependent upon the parent company.

Definition

In studying the structure of our company we agreed to accept the definition of organization given earlier in this book: the tool which a manager has that makes it possible for a group or a team to work together more effectively than they might work alone. To us this definition had a deep significance. We knew that there was considerable talent in the company which was not being utilized to the greatest extent possible. We also recognized that no one can be expert in every specialty of the organization and do everything himself. Therefore the manager must analyze the strengths and weaknesses of his team and attempt to add people in the areas where the group has least competence or least interest. We agreed that we wanted to put together a team of highly experienced people with different specialties. We wanted to organize them properly so that they could work together effectively, knowing what their duties and responsibilities were, what authority they had, and what it was that we were trying to accomplish. If we could do all this, then we should be able to achieve our objectives and achieve them faster, particularly since we were embracing the principles of consultative management and team effort.

Relationship to other elements of management. We recognized that if the four elements of management were to be successfully practiced in our company, they had to be woven together into a fabric of management which would be tailored to fit our needs. We did not want to make our fabric too tight, since we wanted flexibility in order to adjust quickly to meet situations. But at the same time we did not want it so loosely woven that things did not get done or were not done effectively. So in our total effort we kept in mind the relationships between the four elements: planning, organizing, controlling, and motivating. We tested them against each other as we started to define and put in writing just what it was that we intended to do and how we intended to get it done.

Why Organize?

Since we agreed that we organized for the one purpose of reaching our objectives, we had to be goal-oriented. We also agreed that we would be market-oriented; the total effort of the company would be to meet the needs of the marketplace and in doing so to satisfy our customers there. But although marketing and market planning were to be in the forefront, we had to make sure that the other functions did not suffer. The market plan without proper supporting elements would be of no value.

Our problem, then, was to determine what we needed in the way of organization which would effectively execute the plan that we worked out, which in turn would enable us to reach our objectives. Since we would be goal- or objective-oriented, we recognized that while we could not neglect the functions of management in each area of the business, we would not emphasize them as such. We were not going to fall into the old trap of having the finest, most complete functional programs we could develop, without regard to the contribution each one would make toward our objectives. We were determined to be professionally managed, meaning that we would do whatever we had to do and never anything we did not have to do. We would perform only necessary functions, and perform them as simply as we could and at the lowest level of the organization where they could be done effectively.

There was no argument among us that the first element of management was planning. We recognized that, if we did not have a plan, we could not really establish objectives; and, if we had no objectives or purpose, we had no reason to organize. If we didn't know where we were going, we wouldn't know how to organize to get there. Planning and organizing, then, are basic elements of management. They are integrated basic responsibilities of the manager, whether he is the chief executive officer or a department head, and they cannot be delegated.

Since one of our basic objectives was to double our business in five years (actually, we did it in three), we recognized that our structure had to be developed over the long term and would be subject to change. As we grew we had to prepare for the impact of change on our manpower and organization structure—on job duties and responsibilities—just as carefully as we did for the impact of change on our facilities, product development, and market development. Unfortunately, this is not often recognized; yet it is one of the reasons why planning and organizing are so intimately related that they cannot be successfully separated. In planning, what we are really trying to achieve is to reduce the incidence and magnitude of crises as change occurs. We cannot eliminate these, but planning can reduce their frequency and their magnitude. And planning puts us in a position to evaluate their impact quickly when they do occur.

As we started to develop our organization pattern at YAC, the importance of creativity and control, and the proper use of the formal and informal organization (treated in Chapters 2 and 3), were also much in our minds.

What Is Involved?

After much discussion, we came to the conclusion that organization as such is composed of unity of purpose, definition, people, and structure. Organization is a process, a form of planning, not an end in itself. We went into business, not so that we might have an organization, but so that we could serve a purpose, develop a plan to achieve that purpose, and set up an organization to carry it out. Organizing requires the analysis, identification, and definition of work to be performed to accomplish the desired objectives, and it results in a logical grouping of this work for orderly cooperative achievement. Thus the work to be performed, not the structure, is the important element.

In organizing, first we must agree on what it is we are going to do. That is unity of purpose. Second, we must decide what we have to do to achieve this purpose, who will do it, and what authority they will have to carry it out. That is definition. Third, we must determine the number, type, and experience of the employees we will need to carry out the work. That is people. Finally, we must develop an organizational framework that will enhance the teamwork of the group, establish reporting relationships, and provide for a logical chain of command, with a free flow of information which will add to the effectiveness of the total effort. That is structure.

A personal commitment. Once we accepted the definition that management is getting things done through other people, or the more precise definition given in Chapter 3, we agreed that we must personally practice the principles involved. For example, when we gave a man responsibility, we would give him commensurate authority to carry out the responsibility, and we would agree on the results that would be desirable or acceptable. We would not go around him; we would work with him and through him to those levels that report to him. Thus we would practice as well as preach the principles of organizing and organization planning. In our case this was a particularly significant point, since we had not previously had such a commitment.

Guidelines for Organization Planning

Guidelines that should be followed in all companies, whether or not they have a coordinator of organization planning, include these important concepts. First, strive to avoid improperly conceived changes and impulsive experimenting. In the past, managements often experimented with structure and people instead of defining policy, thinking through the problems, and establishing the controls that are essential in good organization, whether it be functional or divisional. Hasty changes that do not get at the cause of a difficulty are upsetting and unrewarding.

Second, be aware of the impact of change not only on people but on structure. Anticipate it if at all possible, remember its effect on procedure and policy, and make certain that, as structure and definition are changed, all the control factors are adjusted also.

Third, keep your structure as simple as possible, with the minimum number of layers for review and approval. Avoid both overburdening and underburdening an individual or group with duties and responsibilities. The span of control and the number of people who can report to any one individual are subjects of much discussion. The best criterion I know of for determining span of control is the number of people the manager can effectively supervise. What do I mean by "effectively supervise"? I mean that he has time to develop, guide, direct, counsel, and control. If he can do this with twenty people reporting to him and still finish his own work, the span of control is twenty. If he can do this with only three people, then it is three. Determining the span of control is not a mathematical process; there is no set formula that I know of which will tell us what it is.

One pattern that the organization planner tries to avoid in developing the structure of the company is the "one-over-one" reporting relationship, in which a member of management has only one other member of management reporting to him. It is generally considered a poor form of organization, except in two instances. One is the situation in which the second man is in training to succeed the first. It should last for only a year or two, since a very difficult state of affairs can result if the man on top cannot restrain himself from going around the man reporting to him. This holds true with all levels of the organization. The other situation in which the one-over-one pattern is justified is the case where the chief executive, for example, removes himself from the scene for a special project. In one instance, the president of a company temporarily retired from direct operating responsibility in order to develop an expansion and acquisition program. For the duration of the project he turned the day-to-day management of the company over to another executive. On the project's conclusion he returned to his normal role in management and instituted a complete review of the organizational structure that his study had shown was necessary.

A fourth guideline for the organization planner is to keep organization planning in tune with growth and change in planning. As he plans for change, he must be very much aware of the impact of change on people. No one likes change. We may not think that we are in the best situation in the world, but once we become used to it and comfortable with it, we would rather stay with it, even though a change might be for the better. Therefore, the planner must try to see that all the people who will be affected by a change have some part in generating it, understand the reasons for it, and recognize that it represents progress. Then they are not surprised, and the philosophy of no surprise is a good one to apply in almost any phase of management. Resistance to change is very real; people instinctively fear it. The planner must understand the logical and emotional aspects of change and be ready to handle both.

Need Versus People Available

In developing the organization structure I recommend that you approach it from a "need" rather than from a "people available" viewpoint. This is a controversial principle, and a tempting one from which to deviate. But, if you focus on your people from the beginning, you tend to adjust away from the ideal to the so-called practical. Frequently the ideal, or the best structure you can develop, is then lost.

To develop the ideal and work toward it is not the

simplest approach, but in my opinion it is by far the best for the long pull. Once the ideal structure has been outlined, fit your people to it as well as possible. No one matches a position perfectly. In some areas of the job his ability will exceed the need; in others it will fall short. One management consultant, William B. Oncken, refers to this situation as the "amoeba" and illustrates it with the diagram shown in Exhibit 6-2. The areas where a man's ability exceeds the need indicate his potential, the areas where his ability is less than the need indicate dimensions for personal development.

You may make some minor adjustments to position descriptions, but they should not be rewritten to fit the individual. If individuals in similar or identical jobs have different amounts of experience, you will undoubtedly grant different degrees of authority to them. There will be gaps in the experience and ability of every man compared with his position description, but let the gaps serve as a built-in personal development program for him. Whoever is assigned to coach the man (and usually the best coach is his immediate superior)

Exhibit 6-2. The amoeba *(from William B. Oncken).*

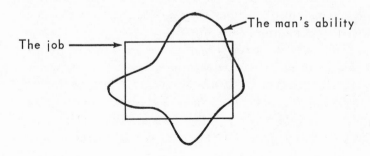

should understand that the gaps are temporary and that his responsibility is to help train the inexperienced man to take over this part of the job. Thus you move toward your ideal organization.

Activity Analysis

One of the prime tools that enables the organization planner to keep the organization simple is the activity analysis. For this purpose it was of major value to us at the YAC Corporation, and it was also an excellent device for involving the organization in depth. It was particularly effective with our people at the clerical levels.

Why an activity analysis? Since one aim of a professionally managed company is that nothing be done which will not recognizably make a contribution toward reaching the objectives, the activity analysis is an aid in pinpointing what needs to be done, and done as simply as possible at the lowest level possible.

What it is. The activity analysis is the procedure that is used to state what action is to be taken, who is involved in the action, what role each person plays in carrying out the action, what he does, and what authority is granted him in doing it.

The result. A simplified, streamlined procedure that spells out exactly what is to be done, where, by whom, in what sequence, and toward what final disposition.

How it can be used. Since it is a specific technique, it is most effectively handled by a specialist trained and experienced in its use. He does not make the analysis on his own but involves at least the key people concerned in deciding what it is they want from the action and how it can best be achieved. The specialist's role is that of coordinator, recorder, question asker, and suggestion maker.

A broad pattern of action in the use of the activity analysis could be as follows:

1. State what basic functions are necessary to carry out the purpose of the business (that is, manufacturing, marketing, finance, and so on).
2. Clearly specify the purpose each is to serve. This is not a casual step in the process. It has been my experience that a carefully thought through statement of purpose is essential to the best results of the organizing function of management. It aids materially in keeping the total effort as simple as possible. It also saves considerable time in determining the need for any proposed action by relating it to how it can help achieve the stated purpose of the function.
3. Study each function and its purpose; decide what elements of each function are needed (for example, in finance: cost accounting, general accounting, budgets, and the like).
4. Determine to what degree each element is needed (for example, in budgets: expense, cash flow, capital expenditure).
5. Make the detailed procedural determination for each segment. Keep it simple.
6. The procedural study could take the following form:

Activity	Position Involved	Action to Be Taken
Capital expenditure budget	Foreman	With the aid of service specialists such as industrial engineers and production control people, compares current capability to produce the forecast product qualities when needed at the desired cost and quality standards. If he has the capability to do so, note on form 1042 and send to his general foreman. If he does not, then, with the aid of the industrial engineer, determine what additional equipment he needs, specify it, justify it economically, enter the data on form 1042, and submit to his general foreman.
	General foreman	Analyzes the 1042 forms submitted to him. Concurs or does not concur with their recommendations. If he does not concur, returns form to the foreman for further study.

This brief example indicates how such a study can be made. When it is completed, you may want to draw up the new simplified procedure in a flow process chart so that the whole action can be carefully examined and traced to make sure it does accomplish its purpose and cannot be further simplified, at least not at this moment.

When approved by those authorized to do so, the new procedure is written up as standard and placed in the looseleaf manual provided for this purpose. Everyone involved follows it; but, if anyone who does not like the new procedure can develop a better one, it will replace the one in use.

The net result. (1) A simplified standard procedure to do the necessary. (2) A clear statement as to who is involved in the execution of the procedure, what responsibility has been delegated to each person, and exactly what authority each one has to carry out this responsibility.

Points to remember. First, if there is doubt as to whether or not a particular action is really necessary or a particular person needs to be involved, leave it or him out. It is much easier to add something than it is to take it away.

Second, verbs are very important, because they denote the quality and nature of the action. For example, "recommend," "concur," "submit," and "approve." It is important to note that only one person or body (the board of directors) has the right of approval and is held accountable for the action.

Third, all forms and procedures should have a specific future review date indicated on them. This forces a review to approve them for an additional specified period of time, simplify them, or eliminate them.

103

Manpower Planning

Although the greatest shortage in today's world is competent manpower, and although the executive search business is still a flourishing one as companies hire recruiting firms to find people for them, it is a growing conviction on the part of most managements that they must develop a program for growing their own executive talent. Not only does such a program insure that people are available when they are needed, but its existence is very important in retaining young talent. Young people who know that there is a formal program for their personal development and a formal procedure through which they will be considered as opportunities arise have a tendency to stay with a company rather than seek advancement by moving around. Probably the Standard Oil Company of Ohio has the most sophisticated approach to this problem in the country today, although it does not stand alone.

The prime factor in manpower planning is that manpower needs must be considered with the same care and thought as needs for products, facilities, markets, money, and the like. As management develops its organizational needs for the future in order to support its program and plans, it designates the people who will be needed. It discovers whether or not the firm has these people and, if not, what it will take to get them. Every member of the management team has a record kept, not only of his experience and age, but of his whole history with the company. His potential for promotion is listed, together with the time that would appear to be needed to prepare him for promotion to a specific job. Men can, of course, be eligible for promotion to more than one position.

In such records the usual designations are "Ready for promotion now," "Ready for promotion in _____ years," or "Not promotable." The record also indicates the man's strengths and weaknesses and the type of personal development he will need before being ready for promotion to other positions. One of the key elements which makes this an effective program is the fact that employees know they are eligible for promotion in any area of the company's activities, not just in their present department. They don't have to depend on something's happening to their immediate superior in order to be promoted.

Obviously the judgments entered in records like these cannot be based on pure opinion. The operation of a personal development program ties in closely with standards of performance and appraisal, which will be discussed in greater detail in Chapter 8.

Individual Manager Development

One of the principles discovered years ago which was particularly valuable to us in the peopling of our growth at YAC is the fact that management development should be tailored to fit the individual's needs. General management development programs that are designed to teach fundamentals to groups are still popular and important. Nevertheless, once these fundamentals have been absorbed, the key to management development is appraisal of an individual's areas of weakness which need to be corrected so that he can improve his performance on his present job. In addition, programs designed to prepare him (such as courses in cost accounting, the fundamentals of finance, or market research) are arranged on the basis of his particular needs. Individual management development programs for every member of management are an essential part of a professionally managed company and should be incorporated in its manpower planning programs.

7

Organization: Job Definition

SUCCESSFUL decentralization requires that every position in the organization have three definitive descriptive elements, so that anyone occupying the job can be fully informed about it. Obviously, one of these is the organization chart itself, which shows the place of the position in the organization structure—to whom the position reports, what positions report to it, and what positions are equal. The second element is the man specification for the position in question, a written document indicating the characteristics of the man considered best suited for the job. These include education, experience, age, health, and any other factors considered relevant. The third document, of course, is the position description itself, which warrants detailed discussion.

Position Descriptions

The position description is a valuable management tool which has fallen into disuse—largely, in my opinion, owing to misuse. One of the failings which we as managers often have is that we attempt to make a particular document, technique, tool, or practice serve more purposes than it should. We expect more of it than should be expected, and the result is that it becomes difficult to maintain and complicated to understand and use.

I do not believe anyone can fault the importance of the simple position description. The basic document consists of four parts: (1) the purpose of the job—why it exists, (2) the scope of the job—the area which it directly influences and is responsible for, (3) the duties and responsibilities assigned the position and the authority granted to carry them out, and (4) the working relationships: To whom does the person occupying the position report? Who reports to him? With whom does he work regularly?

The common fault in the position description is that, in addition to these four elements, we frequently crowd into its policy statements, procedures, standards of performance, and even controls. A second fault is that we tend to make it too specific and too detailed, so that it is obsolete in many areas before it can be typed and distributed. No position is static to the point where full particulars can be given regarding duties and responsibilities. A third fault is that it is frequently not written in order to inform the man about his duties and responsibilities but for some other reason.

At the YAC Corporation, for example, position descriptions had been written in the industrial relations department. Sometimes they were distributed, but more frequently they were not. Their prime purpose was to serve as an important part of the salary-evaluation and rate-structure program. There is nothing wrong with this; yet a position description written well for such a purpose may not serve equally well to inform the incumbent of his duties, responsibilities, and authority. It is better to write two position descriptions, if necessary, and keep things simple.

I believe it is possible to develop a concept of position definition that is complete in itself, yet can be related to the other management tools as part of a total package of definition. Moreover, this type of position definition can be simple to maintain and of great value to the individual. First let us look at the position description itself.

As can be seen in the sample position descriptions at the end of this section, the first part of the description is a simple statement as to why the position was created in the first place. At first you may wonder why this needs to be written, but my experience indicates that it is a very important exercise. When a member of management is asked to begin preparing his own position description by writing the purpose of the position, he immediately picks up his pencil. Strangely enough, however, he seldom moves fast from then on. He rarely has considered exactly why his position exists or what its purpose is. Forcing him to think about it is good in itself.

The second part of the description, the scope of the job, specifies the area of responsibility. This may be a

109

department, a division, or the corporation as a whole.

The third part, covering duties, responsibilities, and authority, is the most difficult section to write. In our discussions at the YAC Corporation we had agreed that every manager does two things: He manages—gets things done through other people—and he operates—does things himself. Therefore, we wanted to break down the responsibilities and duties into management elements and operating elements. We agreed that, when we were managing, we were planning, organizing, controlling, or motivating. A duty or responsibility that could not be classified as one of these was thus an operating element.

We wanted to avoid too great detail, recognizing that the fine points of the action would be covered by procedures and other management tools. We agreed that the duties and responsibilities, particularly in the managerial aspects of the position description, should be confined to simple statements of intent. Here again it was our firm belief that, when people understand the intent of what is wanted, they are much more likely to work ably and well than when they are told exactly what to do. The sample position descriptions show how we carried this out. In describing the management element of planning, for example, it is obvious that, when plans are developed by those who should develop them, and, when policies governing them are written in depth for the organization, we are carrying out the intent of planning. The same holds true for organizing, controlling, and motivating. When it comes to the operating elements, these are the things that the manager does himself, and it is possible to be more specific about them.

In covering the authority granted, we agreed that it should fall into three categories: (*a*) the authority to act and report to no one, as long as it conforms with or is not inconsistent with policy and plan, (*b*) the authority to act provided that the employee tells the people affected by his action what he has done, (*c*) the authority to act only after the proposed plan has been submitted to, and approved by, a designated individual. I have seen four degrees of authority and even five, but these are in my opinion mere splinterings off the other three. For the sake of simplicity as well as effectiveness, I think that three will meet the needs.

The fourth part of the position description, working relationships, states clearly to whom the manager reports, who reports to him, and with whom he works closely and regularly.

Position Description
President and Chief Executive Officer

Purpose: To provide leadership for the company's total activities of a quality and nature that will result in growth, profitability, and continuance, that will render a service to society, and that will provide an opportunity for the people engaged in the operation of the enterprise to develop to their fullest potential and gain a sense of accomplishment.

Scope: The entire company.

Duties, Responsibilities, and Authority:

I. Planning
   A. To develop plans of action, both short- and long-range, that for the company establish objectives, define strategy, and spell out in detail the opera-

111

tional actions which will lead to the meeting of the objectives.

Authority—Prepare and submit to the board of directors for approval.

B. To develop policies for the corporate level that define the limits of action and provide the guidelines for the planning activity.

Authority—Prepare and submit to board for approval.

C. To see that the approved corporate policies are properly interpreted and defined in writing for each area and level of the organization.

Authority—To act.

II. Organizing

A. To develop a plan of organization showing both structure and people needs that is compatible with the plans for the company's growth and development.

Authority—Prepare and submit to board for approval.

B. To develop a management development program that will enable the company to meet its projected manpower needs.

Authority—To act.

C. To develop a plan of organization that will show the current structure of the management organization together with position specifications for each responsibility.

Authority—To act.

III. Controlling

A. To develop for each element of the business performance objectives, both short- and long-range, that will support the company plan.

Authority—To act.

B. To develop systems of controls over the total activities of the company that will permit each responsible person to quickly and accurately measure his accomplishments in relation to his predetermined objectives.

Authority—To act.

IV. Motivating

A. To develop within policy and procedure an effective designation and operation of the philosophy of decentralized decision making.

Authority—To act.

B. To create a working relationship pattern within the company that will attain and maintain a high level of executive and employee morale.

Authority—To act.

C. To see that all areas of the organization receive adequate advice, counsel, assistance, and service to help them attain their objectives and develop to their maximum potential.

Authority—To act.

D. To conduct himself and encourage others to conduct themselves, in a manner that will reflect credit upon the company and on the American system of free enterprise.

Authority—To act.

E. To be responsible for developing, maintaining, and disseminating throughout the company a basic corporate philosophy designed to insure to all employees the maximum degree of personal satisfaction in the performance of their assigned tasks.

Authority—To act.

V. Operating

A. To represent the company to the public, industry,

and government in such a manner as to enhance its reputation.

Authority—To act.

B. To participate directly in affairs of trade associations.

Authority—To act.

VI. Working Relationships
   A. Reports to the board of directors.
   B. Has reporting to him VP–finance, VP–marketing, VP–manufacturing, VP–research and engineering, VP–foreign operations, secretary, VP–personnel, VP–new business.

Position Description
Farm Manager

Location: Farm No. 3.

Department: Production.

Purpose: To manage the production of crops and the development of the land under his jurisdiction in such a manner as to gain optimum yield and returns on investment, both now and in the future. To provide leadership for all people under his supervision of a quality and nature that will encourage them to perform to the best of their ability and to develop to their fullest potential.

Scope: All operations at the location except harvesting.

Duties, Responsibilities, and Authority:

I. Planning
   A. To study all planting, development, and maintenance schedules and plans. To prepare specific

proposals that will lead toward achieving the objectives established for the location, both short and long term.

Authority—Category 3; * submits to VP–farm operations.

B. To see that each manager responsible for a crop or service prepares a detailed plan that will properly support the locations.

Authority—Category 1.

C. To see that approved corporate policies are properly interpreted and defined in writing for each area and level of the organization.

Authority—Category 2; submits to VP–farm operations.

II. Organizing

A. To develop and maintain a plan of organization showing both structure and people needs that is compatible with the plans for the location's growth and development.

Authority—Category 3; submits to VP–farm operations.

B. To develop and implement a management development program for each member of the organization that will enable each man to develop to his fullest potential and that will enable the company to meet its projected manpower needs.

Authority—Category 2; submits to VP–farm operations.

III. Controlling

A. To prepare budgets covering all elements of the operation that will provide for achieving plans and

* See *authority* in the glossary for the key to these categories.

attaining objectives as approved by the board of directors.

Authority—Category 3.

B. To administer all salary and hourly rate structure plans for all employees under jurisdiction.

Authority—Category 2; submits to VP–farm operations.

C. To hold periodic operating committee meetings to review progress and achieve objectives.

Authority—Category 2; submits to VP–farm operations.

D. To prepare and submit to designated parties all specified reports and records covering operations under jurisdiction.

Authority—Category 1.

E. To monitor all work performed to maintain company standards.

Authority—Category 1.

F. To interpret company policy and procedures and maintain conformance in all areas of responsibility. To recommend changes in policy and procedures as they are indicated.

Authority—Category 1.

G. To assist the harvesting manager in the effective performance of his duties.

Authority—Category 3.

H. To develop and implement standards of performance with all members of his organization.

Authority—Category 1.

IV. Motivating

A. To develop and implement within policy and procedure an effective designation and operation of the philosophy of decentralized decision making.

Authority—Category 1.

B. To create a working relationship pattern within the location and between the location and other elements of the company organization that will attain and maintain a high level of morale and co-operation.

Authority—Category 1.

C. To provide all areas of the organization under his jurisdiction with advice and assistance, including formal progress reviews that will aid them in achieving their objectives and develop to their highest potential.

Authority—Category 1.

D. To evidence by personal example a philosophy of work, conduct, and personal development that leads to maximum personal satisfaction and maximum performance of the assigned task.

Authority—Category 1.

V. Operating

A. To requisition or purchase materials and equipment needed to support the plan.

Authority—Category 1.

B. To represent the company in the community with the public, customers, and vendors in such a manner as to enhance the company's reputation.

Authority—Category 1.

C. To inspect all property and facilities to insure proper protection and maintenance.

Authority—Category 1.

VI. Working Relationships

A. Reports to VP—farm operations.

B. Has reporting to him: Assistant farm managers, celery-setting supervisor, service managers, shop supervisor, clerks.

C. Works closely with: Harvesting manager, management committee members, and corporate staff.

Development of Position Descriptions

This book has emphasized that the chief executive officer must be the leader in all elements of management, not only in order to show that he is interested and personally involved, but because he truly must take the initial action. In the matter of position descriptions, for example, the chief executive really is responsible for all the activities of the organization. Since he obviously cannot carry them all out himself, he has to delegate them to others. But the first decisions that must be made before position descriptions can be written by anyone except him are which activities he will retain himself, and which he will assign to others, and to what degree he will delegate them. Therefore, his is the first position description written.

The ideal way is for the chief executive to sit down with his immediate staff and have them help to prepare his description. This not only indicates his direct interest but provides an instructional session in which they learn together the type of thinking that goes into position descriptions and the mechanics of writing and structuring them. Then each member of his staff ideally should meet with his immediate subordinates and prepare his own position description in a similar manner. For example, the chief executive officer delegates to the vice-president of marketing the marketing aspects of the business—making certain reservations, usually in degrees of authority granted. The vice-president of marketing in turn cannot carry out all the phases of marketing himself, so he must delegate to the members of his staff. But here again, they cannot write their position descriptions until he decides what he will retain, what he will delegate, and to what degree he will delegate.

So it goes throughout the organization from the very top to the very bottom. Keep in mind that all descriptions should be simple statements of intent, not detailed instructions. In this form they will be living documents that do not change too frequently and therefore are not impossible to maintain.

Six Tools for Position Definition

The manager has six tools that lend themselves directly to the matter of position definition. The first is the position description which, as just outlined, informs the man of the purpose and scope of his job, the authority he has been granted, and the working relationships he has. Of these the element that is most likely to change is that of authority granted, particularly in the instance where the incumbent lacks the experience to have the full degree of authority which the job carries. Even though the position description makes the intent of the job clear, however, the employee still may not know what results will be expected of him. So the second tool in job definition is standards of performance, which specify the results that will be considered acceptable when the duties and responsibilities are carried out. These results are agreed upon by superior and subordinate and are stated in quantitative terms wherever possible (see Chapter 8).

119

The third tool, policy, provides guidelines, benchmarks, the limiting factors under which a man works. Policies are in written form, expressed as simple statements of intent. They are explained, understood, and accepted by the employee and thus become a part of his position definition.

The fourth tool is the plan itself which, as discussed in Chapters 4 and 5, details step by step the actions that he will take and the timetable for taking them. Since the plan is his operating and working guide, and since he played a major role in developing it, the plan is a part of his position definition.

Fifth are the standard procedures, or standard practice instructions. These are developed by means of the activity-analysis technique described in Chapter 6. They are also in step-by-step form and mark a path through any procedure that we have agreed is essential for conducting the affairs of the business. Everyone must follow them exactly, but, as mentioned earlier, if someone comes up with a better or simpler procedure, all he has to do is get it accepted and then everyone will follow it. Another way of putting it is that a standard procedure is a clear statement of the detailed procedure for carrying out any repetitive action that has been agreed upon as the best way the action can be taken to meet the company's needs.

The sixth and final tool in the matter of position definition is information for control, which is worked out at the same time the position description is prepared, the standards of performance are developed, and the operating plan is accepted. This is the information that the manager needs in order to know whether events are conforming to plan. It must be in the form that he wants it and must be available at the time he wants it— that is, early enough to take corrective action if the plan is not working out. As discussed earlier, information for control should concentrate on the vital few facts he needs to know rather than on the trivial many.[1]

When these six elements are carefully worked out and put in readable and usable form, the manager knows exactly what he is responsible for. He can move forward with confidence in carrying out his duties, and to the maximum degree can exercise the three selfs: self-supervision, self-appraisal, and self-control.

Elements of Position Definition

Position description	Standards of performance	Plan	Policy	Standard procedures	Information for control
Purpose	Agreed-upon acceptable	Objectives, key actions,	Guidelines	Detailed, step-by-	Fast feedback
Scope	results in perform-	and time-table for	Rules of	step procedures	State-
Duties	ance of duties and	accomplishment	game	for carrying out	ments of actions
Responsibilities and authority	responsibilities		Statements of intent	repetitive actions	Results versus plan
Working relationships					

[1] Joseph M. Juran, *Managerial Breakthrough* (New York: McGraw-Hill, 1964).

121

Management Terminology

At the YAC Corporation we found it extremely valuable before preparing position descriptions, standard procedures, and even policy statements to agree upon a vocabulary of frequently used management terms. Any language, particularly English, has many words subject to different interpretations. To reduce the confusion that can easily arise in interpreting written documents, especially when people are working in widely scattered locations, they must have a common understanding of terms.

The glossary in the back of this book is such a vocabulary which was developed for another company's use. It is not intended to be complete or authoritative; it simply lists the definitions that people in the company agreed to use as guides in writing their position descriptions, policies, procedures, and plans. It did much to prevent misunderstanding and to reduce the points of friction which can easily become more serious as time goes on.

Line versus staff. Since one of the most heatedly discussed forms of organization relationship in any company is that of line and staff, let us look at the philosophy behind these concepts. The evolution of management as a profession is taking place in a world of increasingly rapid change in the areas of technology, economics, social and political affairs. In order to perform effectively in the midst of these changes, managers who are directly responsible for activities that further the fundamental purpose of the business require assistance from specialists in the elements of management.

The managers responsible for basic activities, such as operations, sales, and engineering, are known as line managers; those who provide help in the elements of management, such as planning, organizing, and controlling, are known as staff managers.

In the professionally managed company, where nothing is done that does not need doing, a man is hired to direct a service or staff function, such as quality control or market research, only because this function is needed. Therefore, management must make certain that the need is understood, defined, and accepted by the organization. After this is done, the service specialist begins making his contribution in support of those who are fulfilling the basic purpose of the business. I think it is a real mistake to categorize people as either line or staff; I would like to wave a wand and eliminate both terms from the manager's vocabulary. Nevertheless, there they are, and they are unhappy words only because we have made them so. Let's learn to work with them.

The staff specialist analyzes the needs of the business, and after consultation with all the line managers who are affected he develops the simplest policies and procedures he can that utilize the best practices known in his specialty. He presents his recommendations to those who are empowered to revise and approve them, and after approval they become the working procedures and policies for the entire company. The specialist then has the responsibility for coordinating the use of the procedures from a functional authority position, for coaching employees in their use, and for auditing them regularly to make sure that they are being used correctly and are operating effectively.

The authority granted to service or staff people is often a source of misunderstanding. I have seldom, if ever, met anyone whose relationship to an organization was strictly a service one. In nearly every instance he had some direct authority in his own department, and frequently outside it as well, which in itself was line. However, it is important to recognize the difference between direct authority and what the glossary designates as functional authority. The definitions of these terms given there will help to clarify the distinction.

Primary versus secondary authority. At the YAC Corporation we developed what we called primary and secondary authority rather than direct and functional authority. The concepts of primary and secondary authority are extremely valuable in clearing up misunderstandings within a single unit of the organization, between units within a function, and between functions.

For example, take the delegation of authority at different levels of a function. In a professionally managed company which practices the principles of decentralization and accountability, it is important that the relationships between those responsible for a function at the corporate level and those responsible for the same function at the divisional level be clearly spelled out, understood, accepted, and maintained effectively. This is vital if the value of the function is to be maximized at all levels in the organization. Policies and procedures must therefore be developed at the corporate level which meet the needs of corporate as well as divisional management for purposes of control and measurement. In order to make this possible, it is essential that procedures be tailored to fit the basic needs of the business at every level, in a manner which not only conforms to corporate policy but lends itself to effective coordination at each level and between levels. In addition, the special needs of every level must be woven into the procedures in a manner that does not impair their effectiveness.

Therefore, we must fulfill two requirements: We must insure uniformity in adherence to policy and procedures, and we must grant authority commensurate with the necessary accountability at each level and in each organizational unit. Toward this end, every member of a unit must report to the manager of that unit and must be responsible to him for his overall performance. Thus the manager exercises primary authority over the actions taken and the results obtained by each individual in his unit as well as by the unit as a whole.

For those members of the unit whose responsibilities, insofar as they involve policies and procedures, are confined to the unit itself, this presents no problem. But for those whose work relates to policies and procedures which are corporationwide, it is a potential problem. They are accountable to someone outside the unit for effective conformance to corporate policies and procedures. This is known as secondary authority.

Take the controller's function as an example. The relationship between the corporate controller and the division controller would be as follows:

1. The division controller is accountable to the corporate controller for proper adherence to procedures governing the total accounting system for the company. He must perform them to the satisfaction of the corporate controller insofar as accuracy and timing are concerned.

The division controller prepares such additional reports and studies as may be requested by the division manager, but not at the expense of failure to conform to established policies and procedures.

Suggested changes in policy and procedure must be agreed upon by the corporate controller before being made effective.

The division controller is accountable to the division manager insofar as discipline and general performance are concerned. This is known as primary authority.

The person designated to serve as a division controller must be acceptable to both the division manager and the corporate controller.

2. The corporate controller has responsibility for auditing the performance of the division controller and his staff to insure conformance with established policy and procedure. He must evaluate their suitability and effectiveness in meeting the needs of both the divisions and the corporation. When he finds failure to conform, he consults with both the division controller and the division manager and works with them until conformance is achieved.

Special requests by the corporate controller for studies to be made by the division controller must be discussed and agreed upon by the division manager. When completed, they must be reviewed with him before distribution.

In the event of lack of agreement in any of these areas, the controversy is submitted to the proper authority for resolution.

A similar situation exists in the industrial relations function. This is an even more sensitive area, from the standpoint not only of adherence to policy and procedures but also of people's day-to-day working relationships everywhere in the business. In the interests of keeping in close contact with developing situations, pressures can easily arise which would result in having all industrial relations people in the organization report in a direct line to the corporate manager of the function. Yet such a practice would have a highly undesirable effect on managerial team relationships.

The key consideration usually is to insure instant communications when a problem appears. I believe, however, that any such problem can be handled satisfactorily without disturbing important day-to-day relations at the plant and divisional levels. Of course, the maturity of the managers involved and the degree of their professionalism are important factors in the effectiveness with which they will function.

Since the objective of the industrial relations function is to adhere to company policy and procedure and maintain optimum relations between people in all positions, a free-and-easy vertical system of communications can be established within the function. People should be able to use it without fear or favor, even when there are differences of opinion. To promote the principle of no secrets and no surprises in the managerial relationships between functions and levels, it may be helpful to have frequent scheduled and nonscheduled telephone conversations between them. Regular trips by the upper levels to the various locations are also important. In addition, periodic written reports can help to keep those above informed.

Insofar as primary and secondary authorities are concerned, they are the same as those discussed under the controller's function. Again, differences of opinion and interpretation must not remain unresolved for any significant period. If necessary, they must be presented to the proper authority for resolution. There should be no concealment of an unsatisfactory situation regardless of its nature, its cause, or the persons responsible.

8

Standards of Performance and Appraisal

STANDARDS of performance—that very useful tool of management—may be defined as stating the conditions that will exist when a job is satisfactorily done. Standards of performance are known to both superior and subordinate, since they are worked out together prior to the beginning of the activities in question. They not only provide a sound basis for common understanding, but enable the subordinate to do a better job of planning and to work with confidence because he knows what is expected of him.

Resistance to Standards

As a company moves from the free-wheeling, seat-of-the-pants type of management to a more formally organized and control-minded operation, there is often a great deal of resistance to establishing standards. It may arise from a fear of commitment on the part of either superior or subordinate—a reluctance to become too specific about what he wants to accomplish and even how he wants to accomplish it. The failure to utilize this tool is unfortunate, since it is essential if decentralization is to be practiced as a philosophy of management. It is also a natural part of the unit president concept.

Whether we like it or not, or recognize it or not, standards do exist for any position in an organization. We hire a man to do a job, we pay him for doing it, we promote him because he did a good job or an outstanding one, and we remove him if he doesn't perform. All this indicates that there *are* standards, whether they are formal or informal, written or verbal, expressed or implicit. It seems reasonable, then, that we should write down the results that are expected, just as we write down the job's duties, responsibilities, and authority in the position description.

Strange as it may seem, many times it is the superior who is reluctant to establish standards. Often he prefers a moving target so that, no matter how well his subordinate may perform, he can indicate that it wasn't quite what he had in mind. But, if he has something in mind, he should express it. This is only fair, and it is an important part of successful management—particularly when we recognize that our purpose as managers is to help our people develop to their greatest potential.

Just as often, it is the subordinate who is unwilling to commit himself to a standard, perhaps because of general lack of confidence or perhaps because of an unpleasant experience. It may be that in the past his failure to meet his standards for some good reason resulted in punitive action by his superior. Thus subordinates too may prefer a moving target, so that after the fact they can claim that they accomplished their objective even though they did not.

Objectives Versus Standards

There is often confusion between the terms "objectives" and "standards of performance," objectives sometimes being used to designate standards of performance. I have no objection to this, as long as everyone understands what we are talking about. However, I prefer to use objectives in speaking of the targets of the group and standards of performance in speaking of the targets of the group's individual members. Then the sum total of all the individual members' standards of performance equals the group objectives.

The standards of performance established by the head of the group—the department head, for example—will include many of the group's objectives. This is particularly true when he does not make a specific and direct contribution to the objectives. Also, many standards —such as those implicit in budgets—will serve as an individual's standards of performance as well as the group's objectives. All we are trying to do in establishing standards is to agree beforehand upon a result that we want to achieve and whose achievement indicates acceptable performance.

Concrete, Attainable Results

A somewhat longer definition of a standard of performance is that it is a statement of a condition that will exist or not exist, is wanted or not wanted, is acceptable or not acceptable, and is expressed in quantitative and qualitative terms. These terms should not be vague or weasel words such as "adequate," "acceptable," "efficient," and the like. Standards are concrete, attainable results that are agreed to by superior and subordinate before the activity takes place. They are usually stated in four terms: quantity, quality, cost, and time. While it is important that standards be considered in the light of these four dimensions, we should not use any more of them than are necessary to properly qualify the standard and reduce the possibility of misunderstanding.

The common usage of the word "standard" indicates that it is an exact thing, as in engineering standards. But we are not held to this degree of precision in standards of performance; we can have standards even though they may not be exact. They can even be descriptions of past experience, just as long as the superior and subordinate agree on them. This is the important point.

While it is not easy to develop standards for some jobs, it is not nearly as difficult as people will claim. Regardless of the difficulty, the benefits are worth it. Standards provide a common understanding of the results expected among all interested parties. They focus attention on all aspects of the job. They provide a sound basis for performance appraisal. They stimulate self-appraisal, and they set the direction for a man's individual development and progress on his job. They improve attitudes, since they help establish a sound relationship between superior and subordinate. Finally, they tend to raise the general level of performance. One of the surprising features is that when there is a proper climate for the development of standards, a subordinate usually sets higher standards than his superior would. However, if standards proposed by the subordinate do not meet the performance requirement of the action, they must be realistically negotiated upward. The subordinate's acceptance and commitment are essential, and the superior must help him work out a program that will meet the desired result.

Generally accepted characteristics of standards of performance, then, should be as follows: (1) They are jointly developed by a superior and subordinate, and only between the two of them. (2) They are statements of the basic results expected in the performance of an operation. (3) They are worded to prevent misinterpretations—that is, they avoid weasel words. (4) They establish measurements of the quantity and/or quality of the work performed. (5) They are set up in an officially approved form. (6) They are attainable. (7) They are as specific as possible in order to clear up confusion as to authority and responsibility on the part of the individual.

If there are no standards, then the job really has no purpose. Standards can be written for any job unless it lacks purpose.

The Development of Standards

The ideal place to begin the development of stand-ards of performance is with the president and chief executive officer. He has the total responsibility for the efforts of all personnel; and, until he has established his own standards with the aid of his subordinates, they cannot effectively establish theirs. As mentioned earlier, many times the corporate objectives will also be the standards of performance for the chief executive.

Ideally, standards are developed by the manager and his subordinate sitting down together and discussing their jobs. Frequently, however, owing to the pressure of time, the subordinate will prepare his own standards and bring them to his superior for discussion. Either method can be satisfactory. Either promotes reasonable understanding of what is expected on the job, and either provides an opportunity to review the job thoroughly. This review in itself is often worth the whole exercise, since many times misunderstandings develop as to just what the subordinate is responsible for and what author-ity he has. Obviously also, such a review sets the stage for the appraisal interview that takes place at least once a year.

In the first stages of the development of standards, we frequently spend too much time trying to cover every aspect of every position. Actually, there are four to six key elements in any job, and if good standards can be established for these at first, we have made sub-stantial progress. Standards for the other elements can be added as time moves along. The question frequently arises whether to fit standards to the job or to the man. I think it is much more satisfactory to set them for the job, so that the man must grow into the job. This leads to equity, particularly when there are people performing the same or related work, and prevents misunderstanding as to what the final achievement level should be.

Standards should be reviewed at least once a year—and more frequently if there have been important changes in some aspect of the job, if its relationship to other jobs changes, or if a situation arises which makes it impossible to achieve the original standard.

Those Special Jobs

Resistance to establishing standards of performance is found most often in positions that are creative, supportive, and less tangible than those directly related to the manufacture and sale of a product. Yet standards can be established for them also. During the first stages of our development of standards at the YAC Corporation, the head of the advertising department protested rather strongly that his work was creative and that his people could not be measured in the same manner as employees connected with manufacturing, engineering, or sales. He chose his artists as an example, and in the ensuing discussion we asked him what his artists did. They prepared drawings, he said. What for? For illustrating the ads. How many drawings did they prepare for one ad? A good many. How many did they get accepted? Well, they felt that they had done well if they got one in five accepted. Thus we had a standard: Satisfactory performance will have been achieved in relation to the development of sketches and drawings for advertisements if one in five is accepted by authorized persons. Then we asked him how long it took to make a drawing. He said that an artist who prepared a good drawing every two days was performing well. Now we had another standard. Whether or not these standards were right isn't important; the point is that we all agreed on them.

Next in this discussion we turned to the quality of the ad itself. We recognized that it is very difficult to relate direct sales to a particular ad. Nevertheless, we all believed that advertising is important to sales, so we felt that there must be some way of determining whether or not individual ads are effective. We found that our advertising allowances to our distributors included the purchase of certain ads produced in easel form for display on top of the product. Study of a few past advertising campaigns indicated that some ads drew more such orders than others. After much discussion, we agreed upon the number of ads purchased in easel form by the distributor that would indicate the success of the ad—at least, in the eyes of the distributor.

Further analysis along these lines enabled us to establish standards for measuring the results of an individual ad, of a total campaign, and of all the other operations of this department. Included in the standards were such factors as national awards for an ad or a campaign and ratings on recognition by the ultimate consumer in surveys made of magazine advertisements.

In other words, standards can be established for any work done. If they cannot, then there is no need for the work. If there is no way of telling whether a job is well done, why do it at all?

Typical Standards of Performance

Following are examples of well-selected standards of performance for two top-level positions. The first is for the vice-president and general manager of the architectural and construction department of a large hotel chain; the second is for the vice-president of finance of a large, diversified operation.

Performance Standards
Vice-President and General Manager
Architectural and Construction Department

Satisfactory performance has been attained when, in relation to:

I. Planning
    A. Policies are:
        1. Established so that a need does not arise a second time without there being a written policy.
        2. Explained to all department and operating personnel.
        3. Distributed to those affected.
    B. Plans and specifications are completed on schedule.
    C. The building is completed and accepted on schedule and the completed costs of the project do not vary more than 3 percent from the approved authorized expenditure.

D. Each new idea incorporated in the actual design or the construction of a project results in a reduction of cost or a quality improvement.

II. Organizing
   A. Organizational charts and manpower programs have been presented and accepted by the president.
   B. Every position has an approved written position description and man specification.
      1. The approved written position description has been discussed and accepted by the incumbent.
   C. Ninety percent of the approved positions are filled with qualified people.
   D. Questions do not arise a second time regarding the responsibility and authority for making a decision without there being a written policy.
   E. Every position is filled, and appraisal has been made of the incumbent and his assistant with reference to their present position, potential, length of time required to qualify for advancement, and plan of action.

III. Controlling
   A. The annual department budget is completed and accepted by the president within the designated time.
   B. All procedures and schedules are:
      1. In writing accompanied by flow charts.
      2. Prepared as CPM schedules in the case of major architectural and construction projects.
      3. Reviewed once a year for adequacy and simplification.
   C. All projects start with a budget and time schedule and are completed in accordance therewith, maintaining costs within 5 percent of budget.

    D. Accurate comparative overall and unit costs are maintained on each project.

IV. Motivating

    A. Every department member has a personal development program, subject to review once a year, and participates in at least one formal activity a year designed to help him improve a weakness or enhance a strength.

    B. Staff meetings are held once a period and department meetings twice a year, with coordination of all projects on a period basis via published bulletin.

    C. No more than one justifiable complaint per month is received regarding working conditions.

    D. At least one person is formally recognized for outstanding performance each quarter.

V. Operating

    A. Assistance in short- and long-range planning is given to the president and all division vice-presidents as requested.

    B. Communications are maintained on a current basis with management and operations.

    C. Scheduled meetings are attended or an approved alternate is in attendance.

    D. Attendance at one architectural, one construction, and one managerial program a year is maintained.

    E. Appropriate contacts with government and legal authorities are established and maintained whereby required authorizations are received supporting company programs.

    F. Individual association is maintained with recognized professional organizations, societies, and the community to keep abreast of current trends in the architecture and construction profession.

Performance Standards
Vice-President of Finance

Performance will be considered satisfactory when:

I. Planning
   A. *Accounting Procedures.* Accounting procedures for all major accounting applications are in written form by at least September 1, 19—, and have been reviewed and approved by the independent accountants and auditors.
   B. *Chart of Accounts.* The chart of accounts is reviewed with the president annually on or before September 1 for the ensuing year to make certain that its structure satisfies the accounting and reporting needs of the company.
   C. *Budget Plan—Corporate.* The budget plan for the following year is developed in writing to provide for budgeting indirect expenses by periods, is made flexible so that it can be adjusted for changing operating plans and conditions, and is approved by the president.
   D. *Internal Control.* Adequate systems of internal control covering the company operations have been developed in writing and have been received and approved by the auditors.
   E. *Departmental Operating Plan.* A plan for the controller's department designed to support the overall corporate plan and growth is developed in writing, accepted at the annual corporate planning review meeting, and approved by the president and board of directors.
   F. *Company Policies on Accounting Functions.* Corporate policies relating to accounting functions governing all areas of the business are developed

and the need for any policy does not arise a second time without a policy's being in writing.

    G. *Materials and Supplies.* All purchased materials and supplies needed to support operations of the controller's department are always on hand.

II. Organizing

    A. *Organization Plan—Controller's Department.* A plan of organization of the controller's department is developed and submitted at the annual planning and review meeting.

    B. *Manpower Planning Chart.* A manpower planning chart is prepared indicating sources of personnel to support the departmental plan and is submitted at the annual planning and review meeting.

    C. *Staff Development.* A personal development program is prepared for each key man in the controller's department and an orderly plan provides for reviewing the program with each person.

III. Controlling

    A. *Operating Budget—Controller's Department.* Operating budgets for the controller's department are prepared and submitted to the president for approval three weeks before the annual budget review meeting.

    B. *Salary and Wage Review.* All employees receive at least an annual salary review during June of each year and salary adjustments are administered in accordance with corporate policy.

    C. *Reports and Statements.*

        1. All reports issued by the controller's department are prepared and submitted to authorized persons on the date specified or requested.

        2. Errors are not repeated on statements.

        3. All financial statements are prepared in accordance with sound accounting principles.

141

4. Year-end financial statements are approved by the auditors.

5. Tax returns are filed at the right time and in accordance with pertinent law and supporting regulations. (Controversial items are to be brought to the attention of the board of directors and auditors.)

D. *Internal Control.* An internal auditing plan is prepared and approved by the president and auditors and implemented by September 1, 19—.

E. *Accounting Policies.*

1. All requests for interpretation of company accounting procedures or policies are answered within 24 hours.

2. All accounting policies and accounting procedures are reviewed with interested personnel annually.

3. All accounting procedures and policies are approved by the auditors during their annual audit.

F. *Analyses and Special Studies.*

1. *Outside Requests.* Requests for special work or duties are fulfilled on the date required or on the date for which the commitment is made.

2. *Internal Studies.* The controller makes a study in depth of at least three critical or vital areas each year and submits it to the president and the affected personnel for review, study, and appropriate action.

3. *Staff Standards of Performance.* Each key member of the controller's staff has a set of performance standards for his or her job description that has been accepted by the controller and the president.

IV. Motivating

    A. *Staff Job Descriptions—Decentralization.* A job description on each key position in the controller's department is developed by July 1 following adoption of the unit president concept (decentralization).

    B. *Morale and Cooperation.* Not more than two complaints are made regarding the quality or timing of services rendered by the controller's department.

    C. *Progress Reviews—Staff.*

        1. Each employee in the controller's department receives at least one annual progress review of his or her actual performance against standards of performance.

        2. A plan for personal development is prepared in writing stating major strengths and major weaknesses.

    D. *Review of Standards and Job Descriptions.* Job descriptions and related standards of performance for the following year are developed and agreed upon by each staff employee and the controller.

    E. *Company Image.*

        1. Controller attends all public functions or official meetings as requested by president.

        2. Controller participates in at least one full-time community endeavor.

        3. Controller refrains from doing or saying anything, directly or indirectly, which would mar the corporate image in the eyes of business associates or the public.

    F. *Work Philosophy.*

        1. There is no turnover due to working relationships with the controller or his staff.

143

2. Controller is able to promote current staff personnel to fill three of four higher positions as they become available.

Appraisal Against the Standards

Appraisal, which is also known as progress review or performance evaluation, may be defined as the evaluation of a manager's performance for the purpose of improving his work in his present position and increasing his potential for promotion. The cornerstone of appraisal is the objective of helping the man do a better job in the position he now holds. The best proof that an employee is ready to be considered for promotion is that he is doing his present job well.

As with standards of performance, there is nothing new about appraisal. Unfortunately, most appraisal systems are of an informal nature; a manager will say, for example, that he appraises his people all the time. Usually appraisals like this take the form of criticism, or at least concentration on areas of weakness, with no recognition that the man does many things well. It has been said by some who are less than enthusiastic concerning appraisal that the mere fact of being kept on the job should be sufficient to inform a man that he is doing at least satisfactory work. But this is not the point; it is not enough that a man just do satisfactory work. We want him to do outstanding work, or at least excellent work, in his present position, and we want him to prepare for advancement. This cannot be left to chance, nor should it depend on his superior's opinion or whim. It must be put on some formal basis that is recognized and accepted not only by the man but by his peers.

Appraisal is not a sometime or a casual thing; it usually takes place at least once a year and is based on the standards of performance. It is carried out in a confidential manner, without haste or speed, since this is one of the most important times in a man's career. He and his superior should calmly, quietly, and thoroughly review his performance and develop a program to improve his abilities and prepare him for promotion.

The Two Main Approaches

Basically there are two types of appraisal systems: individual and group. Most of the other approaches are some combination of these. In individual appraisal the boss appraises his subordinates, whereas in group appraisal the boss and several of the boss's peers appraise the boss's subordinates. On the individual appraisal basis there are some disadvantages in the superior-subordinate relationship, the chief danger being one of personality conflicts. Nevertheless, I prefer the individual approach. The prime relationship at the workplace is between superior and subordinate; and, if there are any difficulties between the two, they should be ironed out as early as possible.

My chief objection to the group approach is that it tends to reduce the importance of the appraisal in the mind of the superior. It causes him to share a responsibility that should not be shared, since the manager's

most important function is to help his people develop
to their greatest potential. Also, I think that the subordinate should look to his superior for guidance and
help. He should perform as ably as he can to meet the
boss's requirements and needs, which in some cases may
not be compatible with the requirements and needs of
the boss's peers. Divided loyalty and confusion over
standards can result when the man knows that his performance appraisal is dependent on the opinions and
attitudes of others besides his boss. Individual appraisal,
on the other hand, fosters a direct relationship between
superior and subordinate.

An Effective System

The whole appraisal process is conducted to find
equitable answers to the questions, What is this man
doing well? What is he not doing well? What help does
he need? What help will I give him? And what is his
potential for promotion? One very effective system of
appraisal was worked out by James L. Hayes, former
dean of the School of Business of Duquesne University,
Pittsburgh, now president and chief executive officer of
the American Management Association.

The first step in Mr. Hayes's approach is that of
appraisal checkoff. The superior carefully reviews his
subordinate's standards of performance and other supporting data and prepares an evaluation of his actual
performance, identifying areas of strength and of weakness. He makes at least a preliminary list of things that
he thinks he can do or can help the subordinate do in

order to improve performance. If he puts these in writing, he does so informally, jotting down his ideas just fully enough that he can intelligently and objectively discuss the man's performance with him.

In step 2, appraisal review, the superior goes to his own superior and reviews his subordinates' performance and his evaluation of the men. His boss is very careful during this exercise not to voice an opinion or render a judgment but to listen intently. He may then ask the pertinent questions that force his subordinate to think more deeply and perhaps even to modify his conclusions. During this session the superior's superior acquires a sense of the abilities and qualifications of his subordinate's subordinates, so that he is better able to consider them for promotion within his own area or for transfer to a group where they may have greater opportunities.

The third step is the appraisal interview, in which the superior and subordinate sit down together and discuss the results achieved. My favorite approach to this is to ask the man how he is doing and then sit back and listen. He has the same information that I have, perhaps in greater detail and certainly with more substance. If he really believes that I am interested in his personal development and advancement, he will probably tell me more about his performance and more about his needs than I might ever find out on my own. This is a crucial experience, and the superior must be very careful to conduct himself in an interested and convincing manner. He must remember that a man will not knowingly or willingly fashion a club with which he can be beaten.

147

In the fourth step, a personal improvement and development program is planned for the subordinate. It is wise not to select more than one or two areas for study or coaching, as you do not want to discourage him or drown him in this effort. It is important also that he recognize the need and want to participate in such a program, since you cannot develop him but can only help him develop himself. Once the program is agreed upon, it should be turned over to someone in the personnel department to make certain that it actually is carried through.

The fifth step is to review the position description for the subordinate, make any changes that are indicated, and establish standards of performance for the next year.

Sensitive Areas

It is important to note that there is no discussion of salary during the process of appraisal. This is a controversial point. In my experience, however, it is very difficult to talk with a man about his performance and his development when he knows that you are about to tell him whether or not he will get a raise. Money matters will color the whole discussion and rob it of effectiveness. I suggest that salary appraisal come as far away from appraisal for development as it can—that is, six months away.

A part of appraisal which is not specifically discussed with the man is his potential, although it is desirable to find out his interests and preferences. But it is wise not to make any commitments as to the exact route his promotion path may take in the company, since many times factors that are beyond the manager's control will force changes. The subordinate should be made to understand that there are opportunities of a general nature, and that the prime factors in promotion will be how well he performs on his present job and how well he prepares himself for promotion by studying in areas that would be helpful to him.

In the last step of appraisal, the information gained from it is fed into the manpower planning program for the company. The employee's potential ability and his job performance are recorded, and his back-up roles are indicated in the company's various organization replacement charts.

9

Controls: Fast Feedback

PROPERLY designed fast-feedback controls to indicate whether events are conforming to plan are essential in any form of decentralized organization. With them the manager can delegate authority and responsibility without abdicating his own accountability, since they keep him in a position to inspect the performance of his subordinates.

Planning, organizing, controlling, and motivating, the basic elements of management, are interrelated. As shown in Exhibit 9-1, they represent in effect a closed cycle and have a circular flow. Management is a continuing and continuous process: We plan, we organize to accomplish the plan, and we control to make certain that events conform to plan. The compelling motivation which arises from involvement and commitment to the management process, the giving and receiving of good leadership in a stimulating climate, bring results that could not be attained otherwise.

The speed of change today, and the increasing magnitudes of the impact of change, make it more important than ever to spend time and careful thought to understand the purpose of control, to design effective control mechanisms, and to act promptly when these mechanisms warn that there are deviations from the plan. Control is not punitive; if it is used for that purpose, its effectiveness is destroyed. It provides a basis for quick review and corrective action, not for reward and punishment. Obviously reward and punishment are a part of control, since control highlights performance, but they must be a clearly subordinate part. Control is concerned with the performance of people. It can be effective only when it provides a regular means of meas-

Exhibit 9-1. Cycle of management.

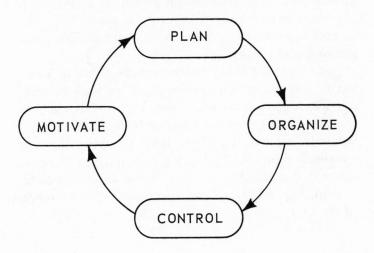

uring performance against the plan. Control check-points must be established at predetermined intervals to insure timely corrective action or a change in plan, if this is indicated.

Control must not be used as a device to centralize decision making. Each decision should be delegated to the lowest level of the organization where it can be handled. The purpose of control is to measure the effectiveness of those decisions.

Control and Decision Making

When sound formal planning exists, and we provide the proper organizational and policy bases for making sound decisions, we are in a better position to implement the principle that the true measuring stick of a decision is its impact upon the future performance of the company. The relationship of control to this very important decision-making process is particularly important when we place it in context with planning, organizing, and motivating.

To select the few key elements that we need to know and to keep sharp control over them, we must be definite about the results we expect. Controls should not provide unneeded information even on vital subjects, but only indicate deviations from the plan. This is sometimes called the "exception principle," since management is notified, not when events are conforming to plan, but only when the operation begins to move off course.

While controls must be designed to suit the needs of all levels of management, special emphasis should be placed on the manager directly responsible for the area involved. He cannot practice self-appraisal, self-supervision, and self-control unless he receives all the information he needs in order to know whether his events are conforming to his plan.

Although we tend to think of controls as specifically designed reporting devices, there is much more to them than this. Almost all aspects of planning, organizing, and even motivating are part of the control function. Here is further evidence that it is very difficult to separate these elements of management in our thinking, since they are intertwined. The plan itself, for example, is a form of control: it predetermines what will be done. In planning, management establishes objectives and spells out how the company will get there and when, what it is going to cost, and who will do what. These are all parts of the control function. Policies, too—the rules of the game, the guidelines to be followed in the management of the business as it moves toward the objectives—are a part of control. Obviously standard procedures also contribute to control, since they describe exactly how the company's repetitive actions are to be carried out. And performance standards belong to the control function in that they specify the results agreed upon between superior and subordinate. Finally, there are the financial controls. Budgets, safeguards against rising costs, and the like plus quality control and statistical analysis, all help to form the control pattern in a company.

Control Over Controls

Management should recognize that controls fall into two classes: the continuing, so-called permanent type and the specialized, temporary control that is instituted for a specific purpose and discarded when the need has passed. A company must be flexible in its approach to the establishment of control information systems and quick to recognize different needs as they develop.

At the YAC Corporation we worked out a simple but efficient system of control over controls, particularly controls involving forms and procedures. All we did when a new one of these was established was to place a date in its upper right-hand corner indicating when it was to be reviewed. If review showed that the form or procedure was still needed, we examined it to see if there was some way of improving or simplifying it, on the basis of our experience with it. Then we established a date for the next review. No date could be set further away than one year, which insured an annual inspection of all corporate forms and procedures to keep them in a healthy condition.

Control and the "Vital Few"

Action based on control information can be much broader than is sometimes realized. When the analytical approach to the solution of problems (shown in Exhibit 9-2) is a part of total management practice, it frequently indicates opportunities that would have gone unrecognized because they challenge the existing ways of doing

Exhibit 9-2. Problem solving through control.

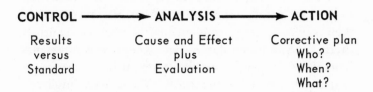

CONTROL ⟶	ANALYSIS ⟶	ACTION
Results versus Standard	Cause and Effect plus Evaluation	Corrective plan Who? When? What?

things. To illustrate this point, here are two examples of the way different companies utilized control information not only to correct bad situations, but to make their total corporate effort more successful than it had been under traditional patterns.

The first took place at the YAC Corporation, where rapid sales growth forced us to enlarge manufacturing facilities greatly in one division of the company. As we worked out ways to handle virtually double our previous volume, we applied the "vital few" principle [1] to our inventory problem. I have always had an aversion to what I call waste space—large areas given over to storerooms—and to substantial investments in inventory. I like to see a rapid inventory turnover even at the risk of a shortage of materials and supplies. In this instance, however, we were increasing our production capacity by so much that there seemed no way to avoid installing a much larger storeroom for parts and materials used in manufacturing. When faced with this fact, we accepted the challenge: Let's take a look at the whole question of manufacturing inventory and just see what we have to do.

[1] Joseph M. Juran, *Managerial Breakthrough* (New York: McGraw-Hill, 1964).

155

Applying the vital few and trivial many concept, we soon discovered that some 25 percent of the items carried in inventory represented about 80 percent of its total value. These were primarily motors, controls, thermostats, and similar rather expensive components. Therefore, 75 percent of the items in inventory represented 20 percent of its value. These were nuts and bolts, washers and screws, simple wiring harnesses, insulating materials, and the like.

Yet we were treating all items in the storeroom in the same manner. All were carefully counted, all were carefully protected, all were issued only upon requisition, and all were accounted for in exactly the same manner. We made an analysis of what it cost us to handle a materials requisition and came up with a surprisingly large dollar figure. Many times, the cost of handling the requisition was far greater than the value of the material issued on it.

The solution became obvious: We placed behind the screen of the storeroom the 25 percent of the materials which represented 80 percent of the value, and we stored the remainder either in open areas to which everyone had free access, or on the assembly lines themselves. Among the questions raised when this solution was first suggested was that of theft. We knew that there would be theft, but we finally decided that a saturation point would soon be reached; there was a limit to just how much of this material anyone would want to take home. As it turned out, we were right. We estimated our loss through pilfering and increased our supplies by that percentage, and on the whole we experienced no great difficulty.

We did not abandon control completely: spot checks were carried out to make certain that pilferage was kept within bounds and that the inventory reflected the value on the books. But the important point was that we materially reduced the space required for the storeroom—in fact, the storeroom for the enlarged capacity was smaller than it had been for the original capacity. We sharply reduced the expenses of handling materials requisitions and of moving materials from the receiving platforms to the storeroom, into the storeroom, and out of the storeroom to the assembly lines. Now many materials went from the receiving platform either direct to the assembly lines or to nearby open-storage areas.

The interest and excitement this created among the people involved led us to develop what we called "tail-gate" storerooms. We took a much sharper look at the rate and time of delivery of incoming materials and tried to arrange it so that receipt coincided more nearly with the actual need on the assembly lines. Obviously there were occasions when this proved almost disastrous—when a truck was late, for example. But the over-all result was that we were able to reduce our investment in inventory by two or three days or a week, which was a plus in our efforts to run a tighter ship.

It is amazing how this ratio between the vital few and the trivial many seems to hold, whether it is applied to materials, reports, responsibilities, or some other area of the business. Again and again we find that the vital few represent 75 or 80 percent of the real value of that area to the organization. For example, another company's use of control information applied the vital-few method in an analysis of all customers for the past five years—their sales volume, the number of orders, the size and value of each order, and the number of calls that the sales engineers made on them. Sure enough, the same ratio appeared: Some 25 percent of the customers were giving the firm 75 to 80 percent of its business, while the large majority produced the small end of the business. Yet, when the sales calls were studied, it was found that the sales engineers were devoting about the same number of calls to the small customers as they were to the large. It is true that the length of their visit may have been much shorter for the small customers; nevertheless, the calls were made. Analysis of the value of the individual orders given by the trivial many showed that in most cases, the company simply could not afford to have them as customers.

Over a period of time, this firm reduced its customer list by 25 percent. It dropped those who could not or would not place larger orders, as well as those who insisted on short-term deliveries to meet their needs and were not willing to pay for this extra service. In due course the company was glad to contribute their business to the competition.

This pruning freed time that was then used to concentrate on servicing the vital few large customers and those small ones who appeared to have high potential. Together they yielded enough additional business to virtually make up the dollar volume that had been lost in removing customers, while profits were markedly increased owing to the size of the orders received. Moreover, this greater concentration on the vital few customers led to such an improved relationship with them

that the company was able to tie its long-term planning
in with theirs. By exchanging information and advice
with them, the firm could plan its growth and facilities
not only to meet the future needs of its vital few customers, but actually to anticipate them. Many times
the company recognized that they were going to need
certain types of materials and facilities before they did.
Thus it reaped the full benefits of the type of analysis
that can be made when planning is approached from a
detailed knowledge of customer needs, present and
future.

Information for Control

As discussed earlier, specifying the information
needed for control is a very important part of the definition of a man's responsibility and authority and the
results expected of him. It is best worked out when he
and his superior review his position description, his
standards of performance, and his plan. This is the time
when they should sit down and designate what he needs
to know, when he needs to know it, and what form he
needs it in so that he can compare his performance with
his standards and his plan. I never deny an accountable
man available information he believes he needs, regardless of what I may think; but I also avoid flooding him
with information.

Information for control is usually of a quantitative
nature. These data are largely alerting or warning types
of control, which report results, deviations from plan,
and critical items that should give the manager a feeling
for what the near future may hold. They could consist

of figures on orders received, backlog, shipments, or waste.

Qualitative controls are also available, usually on a less frequent basis. They include such items as performance reviews, progress reports, and personal inspection trips. Once established, these control devices are subject to constant review to make certain that they continue to provide what the man responsible feels he needs to know. They are not elaborate or complete and can be drawn up quite inexpensively. The important point is that the manager receive the information he wants when he wants it and in a usable form, so that he can take corrective action while the situation is still current, not historical.

Budgets: Two Roles

While it is not the purpose of this book to present an exhaustive study of budgets, they are one of the most common and most useful tools that we have for control. The traditional problem with budgets is that, while they may be carefully prepared and well documented, they are developed some time ahead of the actual application period, frequently as much as two or three months. Therefore, they often do not reflect the actual conditions under which the activities of the business are conducted. Let us take a look at budgets from two distinct viewpoints: that of the financial commitment which the organization makes as to what it will achieve during the fiscal year and that of the budget as a control device.

The Budget as a Financial Commitment

This particular budget is a formal one, prepared in advance of the fiscal year. It represents the best judgment of the group concerning their total income, their total expense, and the net profit they expect. It is usually drawn up in detail for accounts, for divisions, and for the corporation as a whole. It represents a commitment that the organization makes to the board of directors, and through the board to the shareholders. It is my opinion that this budget should never be tampered with, regardless of the changes which may come about. It is up to the organization to do its very best to fulfill the commitment. It is true that many of the assumptions will change, some of them drastically. Nevertheless, the challenge for management is to be creative and innovative enough to fill the gaps that appear, so that the end result—the net profit for the company—can be achieved.

Some organizations are capable of budgeting by periods of time with relative accuracy. Others are not, and it is a common practice for them to construct an average budget. However, averages are rarely indicative of any particular situation; in fact, the average may never exist. I have an aversion to the word "average" and would like to strike it from the vocabulary of the manager. It is often a delusion, since a firm might be doing well on the average and yet be suffering greatly in some specific area. With a budget based on the average, management must be constantly looking behind the figures to see exactly what is the situation.

Therefore, even in making monthly reports to the

board of directors, I like to reconstruct the financial budget to reflect the true conditions that existed insofar as standards are concerned and to compare the actual cost against it. This gives a more accurate picture of what the product mix was, what impact the mix had, what the expense levels were, and how well they are under control. Here, too, there may be deviations of some magnitude due to changes in conditions that were not foreseen. Nevertheless, since this is the financial commitment the company has made, I do not think it should be altered insofar as standards and levels of performance are concerned.

The Budget as a Control Device

From a control viewpoint, budgets are something else. I believe that these have to reflect true working conditions and cost factors, the actual conditions that exist, in terms of both standards and the actual results. This means that the budgets have to be reconstructed by periods and the standards made to reflect actual conditions. For example, if there has been a marked change in costs due to rising materials prices or to labor increases which were not anticipated, the change must be reflected in the budget.

I think it is a grave mistake when we do not place in the hands of our operating personnel in all areas of the business control information which reflects how well they are doing under the specific circumstances they have to face. If we do not do this, then the department head is faced with the constant problem of trying to explain variances from the original financial budget, whereas in some cases of rapid change the financial budget may not be at all indicative of existing conditions. I prefer to leave the explanations of the variance between the actual results and the financial budget to financial people and the general managers. It is important that these variations be examined and the reasons determined and made known. The operating personnel can then be informed of any corrective action that is taken to close the gaps.

Frequently these are upper-level decisions beyond the control of the lower levels. Therefore, I like to have the lower levels of management explain variances between standards which reflect actual conditions and the results they were able to achieve. These are things that they can do something about. Just as I don't believe in setting objectives for people in areas or in classifications that they cannot directly influence, I don't think it desirable for people to be held accountable for results against original standards and activity ratios which could not be achieved or which reflect some broad average that never actually exists. To do so is discouraging and tends to destroy the effectiveness of the budget as a management tool.

As a control device, budgets should be not only variable but variable in what I call the step method. It is seldom that variables can be straight-line—for example, you cannot use half a person or a quarter of a person. Therefore, I like to see budgets developed for various levels of activity—particularly in the people areas, so that they reflect exactly the number of people that will be needed for a given activity. When a variation in activity does occur, there is then no question as to what action should be taken; the only question is one of timing.

Obviously the careful development of controls and control information keeps all performance discussions on a strong factual level, markedly reduces the impact of personal opinions, and minimizes personality conflicts. Control is not an end in itself any more than any other element of management is, so we must keep it in focus and balance. While I stress the "vital few" and "need to know" elements of control, I urge flexibility in the determination of what shall be included.

This, then, is my story—a story of management in action, of involvement and commitment, of team and personal fulfillment. It is the story of a company in which every manager learned to think and act like a president for his area of responsibility, and that is the unit president concept.

Glossary of Management Terms

accept To receive with consent; to take without protest.

accountability The quality or state of being subject to judgment for an action or result which a person has been given authority and responsibility to perform or bring about.

administer To manage or direct the execution of something.

advice Recommendation regarding a decision or course of conduct or action.

advise To give recommendations or provide information.

approve To sanction officially; to accept as satisfactory; to ratify, therefore assuming responsibility.

assist To give support or aid in some undertaking or effort. (No authority over the activity is implied.)

audit A comprehensive, methodical examination and review of a situation, condition, or practice within the enterprise. An audit concludes with a detailed report on findings, with recommendations leading to conformity with, or revision to, established policies, programs, and procedures, if such is indicated or needed.

authority (primary) Power to take action, to require and receive performance of actions by others; the right to direct and give decisions to others. There are three accepted degrees of authority that may be granted:

1. The authority to act and tell no one, as long as the action conforms to, or is not inconsistent with, established policy and is in accordance with or not inconsistent with an approved plan.

2. The authority to act as long as the action conforms to, or is not inconsistent with, established policy and is in accordance with or not inconsistent with the approved plan; *but* with the reservation that the person must inform a specified individual or individuals that such action was taken.

3. The authority to act only after submitting a report on the basis for and nature of the action to a designated person and receiving permission to take action under the conditions designated.

collaborate To work with and act jointly with others.

concur To agree with a position, statement, or action.

conduct To carry on; to have direction of; to direct the execution of.

confer To hold conversations or to exchange ideas or experiences directed toward a position, statement, or action under consideration.

consult To ask the advice or opinion of.

control (noun) A means for measuring and appraising conformance to plan or policy.

control (verb) To measure, interpret, and evaluate actions and results for conformance to plan or policy; also, in some usages, to take corrective action.

coordinate To combine the efforts of separate groups in

accomplishing a specific objective with a minimum of duplication or misdirection of effort. Coordination can be achieved through liaison and communication and can be exercised without having line authority.

correlate To put things in relation to each other; to organize so as to effectively advance a common program.

delegation Assignment to a subordinate of the responsibility and commensurate authority to accomplish an objective or specific result. True delegation exists only when the manager making the delegation confines himself to establishing the objective and standards of performance, to reviewing the results, and to coaching the subordinate in terms of those results and their variance from objectives and performance standards. (A manager may delegate authority to others, but he may not delegate his responsibility and accountability.)

determine To come to a decision concerning an action or proposal; to choose among alternatives; to fix the form of.

develop To lay out or evolve an idea or course of action into a clear, full, and explicit presentation.

development The act, process, or result of developing.

direct To order, instruct, or guide with authority.

direction Guidance or supervision of action.

discuss Same as *confer*.

duty An assigned task.

endorse To express approval of.

establish To set up on a firm basis.

evaluate To weigh and determine the merits of someone or something.

examine To scrutinize; to subject to inquiry or inspection; to test by an appropriate method.

execute To carry to a conclusion.

expedite To accelerate movement or progress.

167

formulate To develop or devise (a plan, policy, or procedure).

function Functions are classified in two ways—as functions of the business and functions of management. Functions of the business are organization units clearly distinguishable from others, such as manufacturing, finance, marketing, engineering, and maintenance. Functions of management include planning, organizing, controlling, and motivating.

functional (secondary) authority The responsibility for developing policy and procedure for the performance of required specialized services or elements of a function wherever they are located within the organization. The purpose of functional authority is to standardize procedure, to enhance the value of specialization, and upon acceptance of the policy and procedure by those empowered to do so, to audit its use to insure conformance.

goal Same as *objective*. ("Goal" may be used to designate a desired result that will take no longer than one year to achieve.)

guidance Conducting or directing along a course of action.

implement To carry out; to give practical effect to and insure actual fulfillment by taking concrete measures.

initiate To originate; to introduce in the first instance; to cause or bring to pass by original act, as in originating a plan, policy, or procedure.

inspect Same as *examine*.

insure To make sure, certain, or safe, usually by a definite review, plan, or action.

interpret To explain; to translate; to give meaning to.

line (operations) In the usage of the word *line* we mean those activities having to do with the basic purpose of the business. Therefore line is defined as units or persons responsible for plans, policies, decision, and action in

168

relation to developing, supplying, and marketing of those products and services for which the company is in business at a profit both now and in the future.

It is recognized that the same type of responsibility exists for the results attained by any unit of the business within its own framework; however, we will not use the word *line* in this instance but the term *direct responsibility*.

maintain To keep up to date or current.

management service An act done for the benefit of another: useful labor that does not directly produce the product of the company, but serves as an auxiliary function to the producing and marketing of services or products for which the company is in business (as differentiated from the services provided to the customers).

monitor To observe or check on a continuing basis.

objective A desired result. (May be defined as a desired result which will take longer than one year to achieve; see *goal*.)

organization Individuals working together in related ways within a specific structure toward a common end.

organization structure The plan of arrangement and relationship of a group of people working toward shared objectives. Its purpose is for people to work together more effectively than they would work alone.

organizing The function of assembling and establishing the human and physical resources of the business in a sound relationship that leads to the effective and economical accomplishment of the objectives of the business. It involves structure, people, definition, and unity of purpose.

policy A definite basis for action or conduct selected from alternatives and in the light of given conditions, to guide and regulate present and future decisions.

position description A document which describes the purpose, scope, duties and responsibilities, authority granted, and working relationships of a position to be occupied by one person.

position specification A document which describes the physical characteristics, knowledge, skill, experience, and education requirements of a person who would be ideally suited to perform a specific job.

plan (verb) To develop a specific course of action expected to achieve a defined and agreed-upon objective.

plan (noun) A detailed and systematic program of action expected to achieve a defined and agreed-upon objective; a path to results.

primary authority See *authority*.

principle A governing law of conduct. A fundamental belief serving as a responsible guide to action; a basis for policy.

procedure A standardized practice; a particular way of doing or of going about the accomplishment of something; a particular specified course of action; a series of steps followed in a regular, orderly, definite way.

program A plan or system for guidance of action leading toward a desired result. (See *plan*.)

provide To make available.

recommend To advise a course of action, or to suggest a course of action for adoption.

represent To act for or in place of; to serve as a counterpart of; to substitute in some capacity for.

responsibility The obligation of the individual to achieve to the best of his ability the assignments given him by the superior to whom he is accountable.

review To go over or examine deliberately.

secondary authority See *functional authority*.

serve To hold an office; to act in a capacity; to discharge a duty or function.

170

service See *management service.*

staff (service) Staff activities are those whose basic purpose is to assist line personnel in the effective performance of their duties. Staff personnel are responsible in the areas of their specialties for developing and recommending policies and procedures and for coordinating (but not directing) the work of the specialty wherever it is found, for purposes of uniformity; for planning its continuing effective use, for auditing its use, and for providing service and assistance in their specialty for all elements of the organization. They are responsible for interpretation of plans, policies, and procedures and may initiate them for submission to line and other staff elements of the business for approval. It is recognized that all elements and positions in the organization may give some services, such as advice, to others from time to time, or may have specific but limited authorities delegated to them dealing directly with the basic purpose of the business. However, these occasional or limited duties shall not alter the designation of *staff* for those whose basic purpose is described in this definition.

standard Any yardstick or measure by which one judges the quality, quantity, or effectiveness of an action.

standard of performance A statement of the conditions that will exist when a job is acceptably done. Whenever possible, the elements of the statement include specific reference to quantity, quality, cost, and time.

submit To present to others for a designated purpose.

support Service, assistance, or supplies provided to another person or department.

survey The action of ascertaining facts regarding conditions, or the condition of something, to provide exact information.

Index

accounting
  performance standards and, 140
acquistions
  as financial objective, 65
activity analysis, 100–103
  defined, 100
  use of, 101–102
  verbs in, 103
"amoeba" situation, 99
appraisal
  defined, 144
  individual or group, 145–146
  sensitive areas in, 148–149
  standards for, 129–149
  two systems of, 145–146
  see also performance standards
appraisal interview, 147
appraisal review, 146–147
authority
  acceptance of, 3
  vs. control, 29

delegation of, 3
position description and, 113–119
primary vs. secondary, 124–126
staff management and, 124

Bennis, Warren G., 31–32, 34–35
boundaries, decision making and, 12–22
budget
  control through, 153, 160–164
  as financial commitment, 161–162
business conditions, planning cycle and, 52–53

centralized operation, change-over to, 7–8
change
  feedback control in, 150–151
  need for, 6–9

organization and, 94
planning and, 27
unit president and, 21
chief executive officer, position
description for, 111–114
"coercion and fear" stage, in
management, 31
common stock, financial objectives and, 66–67
communication
chain of command in, 38
motivation in, 36–39
problem of, 1
company
engineering-oriented vs. marketing-oriented, 51–52, 79,
93
moral code of, 15
company image, professional
standards and, 143
company objectives, change
and, 8–9
see also objectives
conceptual planning, 58–62
defined, 60
control(s)
vs. authority, 29
boundaries of, 13
budget as, 160–164
change and, 151
"control" over, 154
decision making and, 152–
153
defined, 29
fast feedback in, 150–156
information and, 19–20, 159–
160
of inventory, 156
manager and, 153
performance and, 151

performance standards and,
138
planning and, 153
qualitative and quantitative,
160
through budget, 162–164
unit president and, 19–20
"vital few" principle and,
154–159
controller, job definition for,
125–126
Coordinator of Corporate Planning, functions and responsibilities of, 86–88
corporate planning, 86–88
corporate profit growth, as
financial objective, 65
corporate structure, 89–106
see also organization
corporate threats, strategic planning and, 70–71

decentralization, planning and,
43
decision making
boundaries of, 12–22
control and, 152–153
in strategic planning, 72
delegation, by president, 3
Dively, George S., 59–60
diversification, environmental
and business assumptions
in, 75
diversification planning, 73–75
division controller, job definition of, 77–78
division planning, strategic
planning and, 77–78
Duquesne University, 146

engineering, orientation
toward, 51–52, 79, 93

173